PRACTICAL SOCIAL WORK

Series Editor: Jo Campling

BASW

Social work is at an important stage in its development. All professions must be responsive to changing social and economic conditions if they are to meet the needs of those they serve. This series focuses on sound practice and the specific contributions which social workers can make to the well-being of our society.

The British Association of Social Workers has always been conscious of its role in setting guidelines for practice and in seeking to raise professional standards. The conception of the Practical Social Work series arose from a survey of BASW members to discover where they, the practitioners in social work, felt there was the most need for new literature. The response was overwhelming and enthusiastic, and the result is a carefully planned, coherent series of books. The emphasis is firmly on practice set in a theoretical framework. The books will inform, stimulate and promote discussion, thus adding to the further development of skills and high professional standards. All the authors are practitioners and teachers of social work, representing a wide variety of experience.

JO CAMPLING

A list of published titles in this series follows overleaf

Practical Social Work
Series Standing Order ISBN 0–333–69347–7
(*outside North America only*)

You can receive future titles in this series as they are published by placing a standing order. Please contact your bookseller or, in the case of difficulty, write to us at the address below with your name and address, the title of the series and the ISBN quoted above.

Customer Services Department, Macmillan Distribution Ltd
Houndmills, Basingstoke, Hampshire RG21 6XS, England

PRACTICAL SOCIAL WORK

Robert Adams *Social Work and Empowerment*

Sarah Banks *Ethics and Values in Social Work (2nd edn)*

James G. Barber *Beyond Casework*

James G. Barber *Social Work with Addictions*

Peter Beresford and Suzy Croft *Citizen Involvement*

Suzy Braye and Michael Preston-Shoot *Practising Social Work Law (2nd edn)*

Helen Cosis Brown *Social Work and Sexuality*

Alan Butler and Colin Pritchard *Social Work and Mental Illness*

Crescy Cannan, Lynne Berry and Karen Lyons *Social Work and Europe*

Roger Clough *Residential Work*

David M. Cooper and David Ball *Social Work and Child Abuse*

Veronica Coulshed and Audrey Mullender *Management in Social Work (2nd edn)*

Veronica Coulshed and Joan Orme *Social Work Practice: An Introduction (3rd edn)*

Paul Daniel and John Wheeler *Social Work and Local Politics*

Peter R. Day *Sociology in Social Work Practice*

Lena Dominelli *Anti-Racist Social Work (2nd edn)*

Celia Doyle *Working with Abused Children (2nd edn)*

Angela Everitt and Pauline Hardiker *Evaluating for Good Practice*

Angela Everitt, Pauline Hardiker, Jane Littlewood and Audrey Mullender *Applied Research for Better Practice*

Kathy Ford and Alan Jones *Student Supervision*

David Francis and Paul Henderson *Working with Rural Communities*

Alison Froggatt *Family Work with Elderly People*

Danya Glaser and Stephen Frosh *Child Sexual Abuse (2nd edn)*

Gill Gorell Barnes *Working with Families*

Cordelia Grimwood and Ruth Popplestone *Women, Management and Care*

Jalna Hanmer and Daphne Statham *Women and Social Work (2nd edn)*

Tony Jeffs and Mark Smith (eds) *Youth Work*

Michael Kerfoot and Alan Butler *Problems of Childhood and Adolescence*

Joyce Lishman *Communication in Social Work*

Carol Lupton and Terry Gillespie (eds) *Working with Violence*

Mary Marshall and Mary Dixon *Social Work with Older People (3rd edn)*

Paula Nicolson and Rowan Bayne *Applied Psychology for Social Workers (2nd edn)*

Kieran O'Hagan *Crisis Intervention in Social Services*

Michael Oliver and Bob Sapey *Social Work with Disabled People (2nd edn)*

Joan Orme and Bryan Glastonbury *Care Management*

John Pitts *Working with Young Offenders (2nd edn)*

Michael Preston-Shoot *Effective Groupwork*

Peter Raynor, David Smith and Maurice Vanstone *Effective Probation Practice*

Steven Shardlow and Mark Doel *Practice Learning and Teaching*

Carole R. Smith *Social Work with the Dying and Bereaved*

David Smith *Criminology for Social Work*

Christine Stones *Focus on Families*

Neil Thompson *Anti-Discriminatory Practice (3rd edn)*

Neil Thompson, Michael Murphy and Steve Stradling *Dealing with Stress*

Derek Tilbury *Working with Mental Illness*

Alan Twelvetrees *Community Work (3rd edn)*

Hilary Walker and Bill Beaumount (eds) *Working with Offenders*

Youth Work

Edited by

Tony Jeffs and **Mark Smith**

First published 1987 by
MACMILLAN PRESS LTD
Houndmills, Basingstoke, Hampshire RG21 6XS
and London
Companies and representatives
throughout the world

ISBN 0–333–40983–3 hardcover
ISBN 0–333–40984–1 paperback

A catalogue record for this book is available
from the British Library.

13   12   11   10   9
04   03   02

Printed in China

Contents

vi   *Contents*

List of Figures

List of Abbreviations

AEO   Assistant Education Officer
BUPA   British United Provident Association
BYC   British Youth Council
CCETSW   Central Council for Education and Training in
         Social Work
CHE   Community Home (Education)
CPAG   Child Poverty Action Group
CYWU   Community and Youth Workers Union
DEO   District Education Officer
DES   Department of Education and Science
FE   Further Education
GREA   Grant Related Expenditure Assessment
IT   Intermediate Treatment
JNC   Joint Negotiating Committee for Youth Workers
         and Community Centre Wardens
LEA   Local Education Authority
MSC   Manpower Services Commission
NACRO   National Association for the Care and
         Resettlement of Offenders
NAYC   National Association of Youth Clubs
NCVYS   National Council of Voluntary Youth
         Organisations
NISW   National Institute for Social Work
NYB   National Youth Bureau
SER   Social Education Repertoire
YMCA   Young Men's Christian Association
YOP   Youth Opportunities Programme
YTS   Youth Training Scheme

Preface

This book forms part of a larger project: two further texts are in preparation and will be published by Macmillan in the near future. One of these focuses on the management and training of youth workers, the political economy of youth work and the relationship of the work to the local and central state and the other concentrates on young people themselves and the way in which youth work does and can address those forces that structure their life chances. The order of appearance of the books was not predetermined: thanks to the commitment and energy of the contributors, who despite the pressures of heavy workloads and other calls upon their limited time, this book is the first out of the stalls.

The names and reputations of many of the contributors will have, quite rightly, gone before them. They are not merely linked with their employing agencies but also with a wide variety of organisations and activities, and for that reason it is perhaps important to stress at the outset that they are all writing in a personal capacity and any views expressed are their own and not necessarily those of the contributors' current or previous employers. The Introduction and the editing have been the exclusive province of ourselves – neither the contributors nor anyone else should be held responsible for what is clearly our work.

This has been a remarkably enjoyable book to edit. Interested people, too numerous to mention individually, have given generously of their time and energy and without their support and assistance the book would have taken much longer to appear and lost much of its critical edge. To them our thanks.

One person we would like to single out for special thanks, however, is Liz Sim, who at very short notice typed up and made sense of three manuscripts.

TONY JEFFS
MARK SMITH

Introduction

This book has been written largely by practitioners for practitioners, be they social workers, probation officers, community workers or youth workers themselves. As such it concentrates overwhelmingly on the experiences of workers and the ways in which they operate and see the world. This is not a guide to action, a collection of handy hints offering a short course on how to entertain the kids on a Friday night or turn the IT trip into a roaring success; such texts already exist, though how useful these guidebooks prove in practice is a moot point. Neither is it a collection of success stories: rather, it is an attempt by a group of practitioners to offer assessments of elements of their own and others' practices. This makes it somewhat unusual, for though it does not offer a comprehensive insight into the world of youth work it does deal with some of the key elements that characterise the work. The book is organised around a series of roles that practitioners adopt, seek or have imposed upon them. Many of these roles will be familiar ones.

Since the expansion of youth work in the 1960s a great gap has existed in the literature of the subject. No single text has attempted to gather together in any sustained way the divergent experiences of practitioners and this gap has hampered the development of a coherent theory of youth work practice. Compared with the literature of social work, the contrast is immediate.

What is the explanation for the gap? Is it because practitioners are ashamed of their work and wish to keep it hidden from themselves, other welfare professionals and the world at large?

1

We believe there is an element of this, as Tony Taylor hints in Chapter 9. But that is only a small part of the explanation. The problem is more fundamental and is rooted in the absence of a unique youth work theory; one that unambiguously speaks to workers and utilises their insights: a theory that they can both contribute to and draw from. What passes currently for theory does neither of these things, for it has been largely borrowed from other, often inappropriate, sources. Counselling, group-work, community and social work have been raided for theory and guides to practice. In normal circumstances this would be a healthy process, for as Bruce Britton points out in Chapter 2, social work has a great deal to learn from good youth work practice and, as Fran Lacey in Chapter 3 and Gina Ingram in Chapter 8 show, youth work can gain from a similar sharing. However, in practice it has been a debilitating process for youth work.

What we have witnessed has not been a process of integration but of substitution. When practitioners borrow from, for example, counselling, the ideas and modes of working have to be adapted to fit youth work. For that to happen successfully, however, practitioners and trainers require a clear understanding of what youth work is. Sadly, little thinking has addressed this question in recent years. Social workers, community workers and probation officers can all point to key books and ideas that specifically examine what is unique and special about each area of activity. Youth workers cannot. Thus, when ideas are borrowed, they are introduced into a theoretical void. It is not only that ideas cannot be related to an existing theory of youth work, but it is also not possible to relate one idea to another in this context. The fundamental problem is that the youth work galaxy lacks the suns which both illuminate practice and provide the gravitational pull to keep the constituent parts in an ordered relationship.

Like jackdaws, trainers and workers have gathered booty with little thought to the purpose it might serve or the contribution it might make to the construction of a grounded theory of youth work practice. Grounded theory has to be contrasted with grand theory which can be characterised as theory created at a highly abstract conceptual level. Although we would not reject out of hand the value that might result from the construction of such an entity, given the urgency of the need and the depth and range of experiences which practitioners possess, the immediate pay-off and potential of a grounded theory appears to be greater. Grounded theory, with its emphasis upon systematically extracted data and evidence, although not without its critics, does at least promise the practitioner a voice. It places their experiences at the very heart of the activity. This theory must, like any other, amount to a set of assumptions and concepts capable of informing and guiding practice. From this exercise it will, hopefully, not merely offer an account, an explanation, of what exists but will open up a pathway to the construction of models that will assist the creation of a vision of 'what might be' in practice.

The lack of adequate theory has led to a domination by fashions, fads and 'flavours of the month'. Practitioners have been exhausted by the pressure to keep up with these, and disappointed by their inability to integrate them within their practice or to fulfil their promise. Without a core theory based upon the real-life experiences of practitioners there has been no base to which these acquisitions could be fixed.

To hold practitioners responsible for this state of affairs is unwarranted and would certainly not move us any further forward. We will continually relive the failures and false dawns of the past until practitioners gain a voice and a context in which to make theory, and so develop practice. For quite simply no praxis will emerge until we have a theory against which to measure practice, and a body of knowledge drawn from practice against which to measure theory. The conundrum is: which comes first? The answer, of course, is, 'Neither'. Both must move forward simultaneously. When neither exists a start has to be made somewhere and what better than with the workers themselves?

On the evidence of almost two decades it certainly appears futile to await the emergence of a theoretical framework from the academic institutions whose role it is to train and sustain workers. Equally, there seems little justification in looking towards alternative sites such as the National Youth Bureau and the major national youth organisations. Their contribution has, with a handful of notable exceptions, been lamentable. This is not to imply that central organisations cannot make a positive contribution. For example, NAYC has played a key role in stimulating and sustaining elements of the growth in work with girls and young women during the last decade. Given the wider influence of the women's movement and the involvement of women youth workers in that movement it is inevitable that such growth and reorientation would have taken place. However, the added impetus and direction that forums such as the Working with Girls Newsletter provide, and the impact that national workers can make, cannot be denied.

The ability of national organisations to engage with innovatory work has not been encouraging. For example, the recent unhappy history of the Enfranchisement Project within the National Youth Bureau and the current restructuring of that organisation conveys an impression, right or wrong, that it has become a puppet whose strings are pulled by the DES. A mouthpiece for orthodoxy and a graveyard for innovation, as far as the field is concerned, NYB has yet to justify its existence. Youth work, unlike social work, lacks central organisations possessing an authoritative voice, comparable to the National Institute of Social Work and CCETSW, and also the key resource of active research flowing from training agencies and pressure groups such as CPAG, Maternity Alliance and the like. The likelihood of pressure groups arising such as these does not appear imminent. What exist are the generals without armies such as NCVYS and BYC. Representatives of such bodies rush from meeting to meeting posing as the authentic voice of youth work and young people – they are, of course, neither and can never hope to be. Lacking all but the most tenuous links with practitioners and the overwhelming bulk of young people, they are unable to offer sustained opposition to government policy as they are dependent for their own income upon those from whom they wish to extract concessions. Compare this, for example, with CPAG or Shelter, whose research and publications provide the bedrock for all welfare rights and advice workers. Their dialogue with the field is in no way replicated by any youth work organisation. The disappearance of organisations such as CPAG would make it impossible for welfare rights and advice work to continue in any effective form. Clearly, the same could not be said of any of the central government-funded national youth work agencies. This absence of a bureaucratic centre need not be unduly damaging, indeed all this would be of minimal import and concern if there existed an alternative focus for those wanting to make theory and relate it to policy and practice.

The key weakness, when it comes to the heartland of the area of study, remains the appalling lack of scholarship, rigour and commitment on the part of the institutions who have the responsibility for initial and continuing education of full-time workers. Compared to social work, education, probation and even the police and prison services, the literature and research generated by 'academics' has been notable only by its absence. Students and field workers alike struggle to make sense of their practice and career on a diet of ill-digested material culled from the *vox-pop* end of sociology, social policy and psychology and a host of 'practical guides' based on folk wisdom and often little else. What little theoretical literature there is dates from the 1960s and earlier. Valuable in its time, it has now been overtaken by events and the development of theory and practice in other areas. Not until the last few years has a journal of youth work and policy appeared, a newsletter which attempts praxis around work with girls and young women, a series of books addressing youth issues been launched by a major publisher or a national conference drawing together academics, practitioners and policy-makers been attempted. The astounding thing is not so much that these initiatives have been so late in coming but that they have been created at the periphery. This is no accident, for it reflects both a dominant anti-intellectualism within youth work and a reluctance to analyse, as opposed to *record*, practise. A conspiracy of mediocrity has ruled.

The price paid for this has been high. It has been reflected in the lack of confidence of workers when exposed to the market-place of welfare and education, circular debates about direction and purpose, an absence of clearly focused research and an all-pervading atmosphere of individual failure and imperman-ence. John Teasdale and Norman Powell demonstrate in Chapter 6 how youth workers' lack of confidence can lead to their relative reluctance to interact with other professionals. Carol Stone (Chapter 5) explores the pressures that can drive workers on to the safe ground of the youth centre and Frank Booton, in Chapter 7, graphically portrays the impact of such uncertainty and lack of boundary on individual practitioners. None of the authors contributing to this book seriously expects that the years of inertia will be swept away overnight, though it is hoped that it may assist those practitioners and trainers who see the potential of a theory grounded in practice.

Social workers, probation officers, community workers and those in mainstream education will see some familiar themes and concerns in our comments, yet they may have little experience or understanding of youth work. They will certainly be aware that youth work is more than discos and football teams although, as Anne Foreman shows in Chapter 1, this approach still sails along on the crest of a wave. Above and beyond the 'redcoat' orientation lies a world of youth work that proclaims a commitment to social education, preventive intervention, liberation and character-building. With such a variety of approach and rhetoric, tension is inevitable. From Foreman's opening chapter through to Taylor's final piece tension between styles and ideologies emerges as a common theme. It is a tension which practitioners live with constantly and which consensus-minded apparatchiki seek to submerge by recourse to a youth-work language that is rich in ambiguity. Thus the most recent Report on the Youth Service roundly declares that the task of the service is to provide social education (HMSO, 1982, recommendation 5.2), yet makes no serious effort to define what is meant by this term. The label 'social education' is brandished like a *ju-ju* to ward off criticism and justify practice that any reflective assessment would deem at best to be trivial and at worst socially irresponsible. It gives mere contact with young people accreditation as worthwhile in itself. Bill Rosseter makes social education his focus in Chapter 4 and shows that there are practices and ideas associated with the term that transcend the rhetoric. When we begin to look to the practice then there are ample grounds for theory-making. The problem is that the theory we have is free-floating and hence largely irrelevant.

Definitional problems are not restricted to debates about social education, they permeate youth work itself and bedevil the task of identifying its boundaries. The observer of the youth work scene immediately comes face to face with these problems. What is and is not youth work? Which organisations are to be viewed as part of the Youth Service? At what age does youth work begin and when does it cease and become something else? The questions go on, but there seems little value in asking them. Partly because any welfare agency or sphere of activity experiences the same problem in defining its boundary and partly because there can never be any agreement about such boundaries; they will always be contested.

The range of activities that are self-consciously described as youth work is great. Many within the field see this as something that is special to the activity. They are mistaken and it is an error that says much for the isolation of youth work from the wider realm of social policy. For the breadth of activity is no more marked than that, for example, associated with work with the elderly, the unemployed or the disabled.

A danger flows from this apparent concentration upon a group that has only its age in common as much as the danger in talk of the unemployed who, after all, only have their exclusion from paid labour in common. The literature of youth work is awash with crude generalisations about what young people need or want or demand or face or are fighting for. Such undifferentiated use of the term 'youth' leads to a neglect of the dynamic forces of class, race, gender, location and disability. It is no use attempting to overcome this problem, as so much writing does, by simply inserting this litany after every use of the word 'youth' or the term 'young people'. This may salve a few consciences and create an aura of radicalism and ideological purity but, sadly, it achieves nothing. At the risk of appearing repetitive the only way of addressing these issues in the context of youth work resides in interrogating practice as Lacey does here in Chapter 3. From such an interrogation it is hoped that a theory will emerge which genuinely differentiates and shakes off stereotypical assumptions regarding young people.

Young people are not the sole victims of stereotyping. Youth workers too have long been portrayed in ways that perpetuate a series of myths about their personalities, roles and worth. Skip with his pipe and liniment; Akela with her crocodile of cubs; mean, moody but magnificent street-wise Col boldly going where detached workers have boldly gone before; Cliff, Sue and God – The Team; Jackie, all fag ash and sympathy. The stereotypes are legion. What they portray is someting of the breadth of youth work provision. What they betray is the relative sophistication of much youth work practice. The stereotypes are recalled not for the imprint they make on personality but as vague recollections of eccentricity.

Already one can hear from the casual reader of the chapter list the accusation that this book will reinforce old or create new stereotypes of youth workers. Of course this accusation may have a certain justification for we chose the titles quite consciously to expose areas of practice and styles of work and to create an environment for contributors to reflect upon them. Many other images could have been conjured up for this purpose: the youth worker as pastor, earth mother or father, seducer, exploiter, template, manager, proprietor, counsellor. The list is limitless because youth work attracts as wide a variety of individuals from diverse backgrounds as any other occupation. However, this is a partial and potentially dangerous explanation that leads to a belief that success or failure is predicated upon the personality of the worker. As a number of the contributors show, it is the conflicting expectations, diverse settings and above all else the absence of consensus regarding the role, function and *raison d'être* of youth work that create tensions and ambiguity in the minds of workers, trainers and policy-makers. It is ridiculous to bemoan this lack of consensus. All attempts – of which there are many – to create one have failed and will fail, and sitting around waiting for the next decennial government report *à la* Albermarle, Milson-Fairburn, or Thompson in the hope that it will untie the Gordian Knot is futile. Youth work must accept that it is an essentially contested area as is any other arena of educational or welfare endeavour.

Once this is accepted as the backcloth of activity it is possible to make some progress. Within any role there exist contradictions. These can be positively or negatively exploited. Ingram shows in Chapter 8 – in what may prove to be a seminal contribution to the literature of youth work – that even those roles which most of us would see as potentially debilitating and antipathetic to youth work traditions can be reshaped and interpreted to the benefit of young people and practitioners. In this sense our choice of chapter headings has proved irrelevant. For contributors have grasped the contradictions and demonstrated the power of reflection and theory-making to unmask the limitations and construct a liberating practice.

A book written by contributors scattered around the United Kingdom, many of whom never having met one another, is clearly likely to contain inconsistencies and ideological differences. As we have already implied, we do not see this as a weakness but rather as a strength. Nevertheless there is an underlying theme and perhaps most importantly a pervading air of optimism and sense of excitement at the potential of youth work to make a positive contribution to welfare and educational practice and thinking. Foreman in Chapter 1 explores the impact on the practitioner of the pressure to offer young people a diet of entertainment and little else. She argues that there is a fundamental incompatability between the roles of youth worker and redcoat. Drawing upon this discussion Foreman proceeds to outline how the redcoat style can be resisted and a more developmental approach constructed.

Intervention in the juvenile justice system offers the opportunity for innovation by drawing together practices that have often been viewed as the preserve of either youth workers or social workers. Britton, drawing on his experience of working within the Scottish system, provides us in Chapter 2 with an account of one such attempt at integration. He shows that it is possible to work with young people in a way that respects their desire to exercise more control over their lives. By using the expressed needs of the young people as the axis around which intervention takes place, a sustained dialogue between workers and managers in a number of agencies can be generated.

In contrast, Lacey makes community groups the focus of intervention in Chapter 3. Her discussion reflects a desire to strengthen the ability of local people to create opportunities for young people to organise their own provisions. This carries with it the danger of conflict in the neighbourhood which can divide along lines not only of age but also, as Lacey shows, of gender, race and class. She illustrates how these can be confronted and existing arrangements relating to the distribution of power and resources be challenged and modified.

'First and foremost youth workers are educators.' Uncompromisingly, Rosseter begins Chapter 4 by asserting that all other roles are secondary. He explores the implications of this position and the contribution that informal educators can make to the social and political education of young people. Whilst the rhetoric and 'officialese' of youth work abounds with references to social education, the reality of practice, as Foreman has indicated, often dances to a different tune. Rosseter examines the theory, but most importantly indicates how in some way it may inform day-to-day work with young people.

Practitioners complain frequently about the volume of administrative and menial work that they feel they are required to perform. Bookkeeper, stock controller, receptionist, caretaker – all these roles, we are told, deflect the practitioner from the real task of 'social education'. Stone outlines in Chapter 5 the pressures that can contribute to this but she does not leave it there. Using a number of case studies she confronts the reader not only with the traditional explanation for this avoidance of the central tasks but also unmasks the hidden agenda of practitioner-collusion with this retreat from intervention.

Only a small minority of young people ever become entangled within the web of the juvenile justice system. Which is fortunate, because few youth workers – and, one suspects, many allied professionals – barely grasp the legal complexities and emotional and personal toll that involvement extracts from those caught up within it. Teasdale and Powell have considerable experience of engagement with this unremitting system; they offer an insight into this jungle in Chapter 6, and, like Britton before them, indicate ways in which practitioners may intervene or not in a developmental and non-stigmatising fashion.

Fads and fashions ebb and flow through the literature and discourse of welfare professionals and youth workers are not immune from such contagion. 'Burn out' has considerable current cachet, yet beneath the trivial and melodramatic use of this term lurks a painful reality for an unfortunate few. Through the use of case study material Booton conveys in Chapter 7 the impact of the phenomenon and some factors that contribute towards the creation of a casualty.

Entrepreneurs, bankers, competitors and markets – these are words not readily associated with youth work. In Chapter 8, which stands many preconceptions on their heads, Ingram forces us all to confront the reality of power relationships. Using the language of economics she shows how progressive practice can be wrought, and with considered reference to her own experience transcends the limitations of the 'dismal science'. This chapter gives grounds for optimism – Ingram and her colleagues have achieved considerable gains for young people and enabled them to exercise power in their own interests.

Lastly, Taylor, in Chapter 9, a consciously polemic chapter, argues a convincing case for reconstructing traditional notions of 'character building' within a socialist framework. For too long socialists have hidden behind a mask of liberal rhetoric and libertarian practice, ashamed to present in clear and accessible language a vision of what might be. Avoiding the anhistorical approach Taylor accounts for the resilience and adaptability of conservative practice. In so doing he illuminates the essential flaws of the 'social democratic' model which self-consciously assumed its ascendency.

These contributions are offered in the hope that they will stimulate both practitioners and trainers within youth work and outside to address the everyday experience of working with young people. Their originality lies in the contributors' ability to make grounded theory and, against considerable odds, to apply it. That is why, although this book is not a collection of success stories, it is nevertheless a contribution permeated with optimism.

1

Youth Workers as Redcoats

ANNE FOREMAN

Scratch the surface of any youth worker and chances are you will find a hint of a redcoat underneath. Anyone who has experienced the full force of an enthusiastic redcoat in action will not deny that they share more than a few similarities with their youth work counterparts. Redcoats are easily identified by their uniform for a start, and their faces bear the fixed smile of the entertainer. Week in, week out they offer their programme, revamped occasionally in response to the latest trends, and oh! how they encourage you, urge you even, to join in. Participation is also the name of their game. Add to this an obsession with winning contests, a fixation with numbers underpinned by a desire to keep the management happy, and the distinctions between youth workers and redcoats become decidedly blurred. Exchange the uniform for the familiar identikit youth worker one, the setting from a camp to a club and those distinctions evaporate.

If this is so, then does it matter? After all, some of the similarities are harmless enough. Activities, we are told, are a means to an end, merely a tool for working with people and can be challenging and fun into the bargain. Taking part is surely better than doing nothing, and anyway what's wrong with the entertainment ethos? The answer, of course, is 'Nothing', except that it is not youth work. There is, in fact, a fundamental incompatability between the roles of youth worker and redcoat in that the former requires an appreciation of the social and political influences that affect the situation of young people and the latter only the presence of young people themselves.

12

Leisure is at the heart of the evolution of the redcoat style and many equate leisure with entertainment. The arena for social education in the Youth Service has been and is the leisure time of young people and this has led to a blurring of the redcoat and youth worker roles. The informal setting of social education lends itself to being practised under the aegis of entertainment, which in turn lends itself to the redcoat style. The redcoat style belies the true nature of the work and can obscure it completely if not checked.

Leisure and the redcoat style

The Youth Service, since its inception in the late nineteenth century, through its formative years and up to the present day has concerned itself with young people's leisure time. Indeed, the philanthropic aims of early youth work were largely a response to the growth in the leisure time of young people that accompanied industrialisation and a concern about the use to which it was put.

Young people affected most by the changes in society that industrialisation brought were mainly working-class and the Service was thus made up of two clearly-defined social groups. Since youth work was initially voluntary, its practitioners were those possessed of a combination of power, affluence and a social conscience, often rooted in religious conviction, so conversion figured strongly in early youth work. Conversion not only to Christianity, but to the notion of 'better', that is, more middle-class standards, attitudes and values. It can be argued that things have not changed significantly, and certainly the fabric of current youth work practice remains interwoven with the threads of conversion.

Allied with a concern for the purposeful use of leisure time was another for improving the standard of health of the population, which paved the way for the emphasis on the benefits of physical activities that characterised the youth work of the time. As the personal development of young people was enhanced by such pursuits, this fostered the belief that it was the activities themselves that produced changes in young people. Hence outdoor pursuits became the arena for social education, and fresh air became endowed with beneficial character-building properties.

The development of statutory as well as voluntary youth work saw the Service become an integral part of the education system and hence many full-time youth workers in the statutory sector were teacher-trained. Thus emphasis on instruction in the purposeful use of leisure time combined with emphasis on physical activities became the hallmark of youth work. It continued to be a service provided by adults for young people based on the adults' understanding of what young people needed or required. Not until the Albermarle Report (HMSO, 1960) were the needs of young people looked at objectively as a major issue. The report marked a watershed in the development of youth work in that it both reinforced the existing role of the Youth Service and established new trends in working with young people. In establishing that the concern of the Youth Service was with the 'whole' young person – his or her physical and emotional and personal development – the report was a major factor in determining the shift away from seeing the Youth Service as being solely concerned with leisure pursuits. For example, it mooted the idea that young people be partners in the Youth Service, that counselling services be developed, that links be forged with unattached young people, and that controversial topics such as religion, politics and industrial relations be explored.

The development of the redcoat style

Post-Albermarle youth work saw what John Eggleston has described as an expansionist era (1960–65) preceeding an experimental phase (1965–72) (1976, p. 193). Hardly a fertile breeding ground for the purveyors of the recoat style? What factors, then, encouraged the style to develop? The Youth Service reflects the prevailing social and political trends of society, and the 1960s saw adolescents become an ever more significant consumer group. This expansion meant that the Youth Service saw itself as competing more intensely with commercial organisations in leisure provision for the young.

The Youth Service, by opting to compete and provide 'something for everyone', reinforced the redcoat style.

Intensification of the redcoat style served to deflect attention away from the primary task of youth work, that of social education; with the result that social education has not been well enough defined in practice. Theory abounds and a great deal of energy is expended on the perennial debate of social education versus social control. This, when the rhetoric is swept away, appears to boil down to the fact that social education equals social control, therefore thinking youth workers should have no truck with it. A specious argument that serves more to salve the individual conscience than to further the cause of social education and, moreover, pays scant regard to either the developmental needs or the aspirations of young people. A surfeit of invective about what youth work cannot achieve has met with a dearth of evidence of what it can and does achieve. This has led to youth work, particularly centre- or club-based youth work, being undervalued and perceived by many purely as an alternative leisure service for those who cannot afford the 'real', that is, commercial, thing. There is plenty of good practice around, both traditional and innovative, but youth workers are diffident about offering examples of their work and the resultant absence of social education in practice paves the way for the redcoat style to reign.

Management and the redcoat style

The redcoat style has been further influenced by the increased attention given to management within the Youth Service. Although the Service has always been managed, a recent emphasis on the quality of this has resulted in management within the Service being examined and found wanting and this situation has fostered the insidious notion that good management alone is the panacea for whatever ails the Youth Service. The increasing use of management techniques without adequate clarification or understanding of their purpose has led to some workers stating with feeling that line management has been imposed upon them. This leads to their feeling constrained by management rather than empowered by it; workers feel their autonomy threatened. Within an atmosphere of control the tangibles of 'who and how many did what' are the main focal points. This fosters the redcoat style since it is simpler after all to evaluate a borough tournament, for example, than to monitor the attempts to truly increase member involvement in running a club. For many workers, resistance to management seems to stem from the fact that, for them, management itself is a perjorative term, carrying with it the implication that management is inhumane *per se* and as such is incongruent with the nature of youth work. This situation will remain true for many until the nettle of what constitutes good and appropriate management within the Youth Service is firmly grasped by the training agencies, workers and officers alike.

The changing face of leisure

Having outlined the background that fostered the development of the redcoat style, it is important also to consider the nature of the leisure time within which it is located. Until the late 1970s, whatever the style of youth work, the leisure time in which it was practised meant one thing: time away from school or work. This concept of leisure is no longer valid for large numbers of young people today. The spectre of unemployment looms larger over the young than over any other members of society apart from the elderly, and ensures that for many of them *most* of their time is leisure time. The Thompson Report acknowledges that this 'enforced' leisure time is intrinsically different from the leisure time of those with work: 'The true meaning of leisure can hardly exist outside the framework of work, and denying young people the possibility of work may in a sense also deprive them of the possibility of real leisure' (HMSO, 1982, p. 17). The 1980s have witnessed a situation where young people have more leisure time than ever before and the maxim that the devil makes work for idle hands is one imprinted in the minds of many involved in youth work. Thus we come full circle to the original concern of early youth work: the purposeful use of increased leisure time.

Being a redcoat can seriously damage your youth work

Although the redcoat style of youth work will not of itself bring the Youth Service tumbling down, clubs still get run, tournaments played, discos danced, members' committees elected and coffee bars run. Nevertheless, being a redcoat can seriously damage your youth work. For the redcoat style is essentially one of provision: a programme of various activities is offered and if there are not enough takers then the programme is revamped and offered again. Then when the mix is right and there are enough takers it is considered successful in terms of results and numbers and slowly the social education content gets overlooked. Thus workers slowly and imperceptibly get drawn into the redcoat style.

Purveyors of the redcoat style have not formed part of the vanguard of any significant developments in youth work over the last few years. The impetus for developments in work with the young unemployed, in black youth work, in work with girls and young women, in work with juniors, has come from youth workers rather than from redcoats. Youth workers who have listened and responded to the developmental needs of the young people they work with. A note of caution here, though, as being innovative of itself does not provide an immunity against the redcoat style. A critical look at what is happening in the fields of work with the unemployed or with girls, for example, reveals that the redcoat style is slowly but surely creeping in.

Nevertheless a significant feature of such work has been that it has acknowledged the changing social climate and has shifted away from the earlier person-centred approach to social education aimed at maximising individual fulfilment, and towards working collectively around issues of concern to young people. In sharp contrast, the redcoat style constitutes a recipe for a Youth Service in which no ripples are made, a recipe for stagnation: a leisure service with little chance of fostering young people's critical involvement in their community. The current political and economic climate ensures cutbacks, and restrictions constrain what is being done with and for young people. Within this context a Youth Service that is perceived merely as an alternative leisure service is particularly vulnerable to cuts in resources.

Meeting myths

Many youth workers, full-time and part-time, do not develop into redcoats at all, but they start out that way. They are attracted into a service that provides them with an audience and allows them free reign. Other youth workers may not start out wanting to be redcoats, but can find themselves absorbed into the style given the conditions described. One reason that the redcoat style rules, even if it is by default, is that once in the field, youth workers meet myths and myths play a major role in consolidating the style. Take, for example, the oldest chestnut of all: the numbers game. Much is made of this game and like most myths it has its seeds in the ground of reality. Numbers are important; to suggest otherwise is naïve. For many, numbers remain the yardstick by which results are measured and resources allocated. However, too many workers contribute to the power of this myth by not attempting to influence the way resources, whether that means funding on a large scale or an extra paid session for a one-night-a-week club, are allocated. Similarly with results; if numbers dominate the criteria for measuring results, then it is the responsibility of the youth worker to come up with additional relevant criteria: the aims of the work, who was involved, how decisions were made, what was the level of experience offered, what were the good bits, the not so good, and why? In the absence of any alternative yardstick for distributing resources and measuring results, it is not surprising that numbers prevail. The more aspects of the work that are included for consideration, the more likely that the underlying philosophy of youth work will be the point of focus. Entertainment provision and numbers then become but one part of the spectrum.

This implies there is an instant means of counteracting one of the most pervading of myths and, of course, there is no such thing. Attempts to dispel myths involve influencing policy, which takes time and not a little patience. It requires an understanding of the system involved and knowing where to raise the issues; getting oneself on to a relative committee; establishing links with people in the community; and harnessing the support of sympathetic councillors, youth officers and colleagues. Above all, it means holding fast to one's own philosophy and sense of vision, for that is what will strengthen resolve when resistance is met at every turn, or the minutae of routine tasks associated with youth work become discouraging.

For those workers who feel that influencing policy is not part of their remit, that the day-to-day running of the club is work enough, it is suggested that such an attitude is the first step down the narrow path that is the redcoat style. Unless workers play an active part in influencing policy and decision-making, then increasingly it will be done by others on their behalf; others for whom the social education role of youth work may be obscured by pressure to streamline resources. Consider, for example, the increasing number of authorities where the Youth and Community Service has been usurped by Arts and Libraries Departments, or Leisure and Recreational Departments, from its place within Education.

Challenging myths does not, of course, always explode them, but it does create space for manoeuvre and helps push out the sometimes artificial boundaries they impose on youth work. This sort of approach will not necessarily make life easy for workers or youth officers, but of all the motivating forces that lead people into youth work, making life easy for youth officers is not one frequently encountered! Officers worth their salt would encourage such an approach in any case.

Resisting the redcoat style

If the redcoat style is easy to slip into, but damaging to youth work, how may it be resisted? One way is to argue the case for youth work with honesty and clarity. Too often the aims of youth work are not made explicit and then the work gets wrapped up and offered purely as a leisure activity, as if that were the only way to arouse the interest of young people. When this is the case, small wonder that the style of working adapts itself to the way the work is presented. But short of a large sign over the club door: 'Social education this way' – in what practical ways is it possible to present the case for youth work and to be open about the nature of the work? The examples outlined here are based on the experience of workers involved in centre-based youth work. Since they are rooted in everyday practice, they are by their nature parochial; they may also appear obvious. However, it is frequently the obvious that can get overlooked in the daily round.

First, do people, including club members or users, know 'what the club is about'? Where it fits into the general scheme of things? What its aims are, how those aims were agreed? What impression do people get coming into the club for the first time? The messages received from the look and feel of a place can be powerful ones in distinguishing a youth club from commercial provision. (And, in response to the cynics, no reference is being made to the standard of decor or furnishings.) The youth worker must ensure that 'what the club is about' is known, and one of the best places to share this information can be the management committee.

Sharing information with the management or advisory committee is one of the most effective ways of presenting the case for youth work and gaining support for trying new approaches. Experience of working with a Management Committee shows that the more they find out about the way the youth work happens, the more interested and supportive they become. Make full use of the youth worker's report; it can be so much more than an up-date of what has happened since the last meeting. The report to a management committee can take several forms. Sometimes a straightforward written report on one facet – working with girls, for example, or training, or the planning of an open meeting. Reports may be presented by different workers describing their work, or by club members reporting their involvement in particular aspects of the club. Still others can focus on issues such as unemployment or the way decisions are made in the club. It will be trial and error at first, not least because it can be difficult to articulate what may have become an instinctive method of working, and some reports will inevitably be better than others. But though the reports will be varied, what they have in common is an attempt to convey the reasons why the club is trying to make something happen. Why the involvement of young people, what would they gain from involvement? Why work for a better deal for girls and young women? Why try and do youth work outside the club or in the daytime? Why spend money on improving the lighting and making space for a quiet comfortable place to sit? Colleagues who have used a similar approach with their management committees agree that the discussion about the how and why of youth work both generates interest and ensures that fundamental aspects of the work are recognised, written into the minutes and accepted as the 'business' of the club.

In addition, when people are aware of the aims of one's work they are much more likely to be supportive in trying something new. If the 'something new' also happens to be 'new' within the current thinking and practice of your local authority, then the backing of an interested management committee can be support indeed. If a piece of work is likely to be viewed as contentious, then it is worth trying to get support for a given period of time. Be prepared, though, to outline objectives and report back. In this way new work can be put on the agenda, be discussed and gradually absorbed into the mainstream. Additional backing for new work can come through the judicious use of 'official' material. Using Thompson, for example, to support a case for political education or work outside the age range set down by the local authority can lend weight to an argument. Such support has the added virtue of demonstrating that these issues are not merely a personal hobby horse, but a legitimate part of mainstream youth work.

New projects can have a ripple effect and filter through to other areas of work. Initial attempts at encouraging greater participation by girls and young women, for example, has, over a period of time, led to our management committee making recommendations for changes in their constitution to reflect a commitment to working with girls. The access to and appropriateness of existing resources for girls is being considered and the current job description of the full-time youth worker is being redefined to incorporate work with girls. Modest changes, it is true, but tangible none the less and significant, since getting things written down in this way ensures that such issues do not go away and that they are not dependent upon the personal interest and energy of individual workers. Getting things written down also provides a base from which work can develop. Other work that has developed in similar vein has been daytime youth work, working with juniors and different use of instructor sessions, in order to introduce a wider variety of experiences and skills, rather than coaching for the already proficient.

Arguing the case for youth work in this way not only leads to recognition for the work but also serves to sharpen the distinction between the social education content of youth work and the mere leisure provision offered by redcoats. In addition, it can focus on the social and political influences affecting young people so that a concern such as unemployment, for example, can begin to be seen as a public issue rather than as an individual personal failure.

What if there is neither a supportive management committee nor a sympathetic youth officer? How then to resist becoming a redcoat? One option here is to carve a space for the innovative alongside what is regarded as tried and true. In other words, deliver the goods expected in terms of numbers for example, but in addition create space for an alternative approach. This may necessitate a search for volunteer workers if there is no way such work can be done from existing resources. Easier said than done, but such work has developed and flourished in an initially unsympathetic atmosphere. One concern here, of course, is that individual workers have to consider the political expediency of apparently offering more services from existing or contracting resources.

The recognition of other workers in the field is also valuable. It is the discussion with other workers that generates the support, encouragement, challenge and criticism necessary for developmental youth work to thrive. Finding the time is hard but worthwhile, for the reverse side of the valuable coin of autonomy is isolation, which in turn can lead to staleness. Being aware of what other workers are doing can have a practical use too. Being able to illustrate that the precedent has been set can be a useful backing for a particular area of work it is hoped to develop. It can also be effective in appealing to those people for whom being seen to be aware of current trends is important.

Redcoats, youth workers and young people

It has been suggested earlier that there is a fundamental incompatability between the roles of youth worker and redcoat, since the former requires an interventionist appreciation of the social and political influences that shape the experience of young people, which the latter avoids. But what is the impact of these different ways of working with young people themselves?

Central to the redcoat style is the provision of a range of activities that young people can tap into or not as they choose. The activities themselves may prove enjoyable and rewarding. So far, so good. And yet the impact of such provision on young people is limited by its very nature to being no more than an enjoyable way to pass time. Instead of being seen as a starting point for working with young people, the redcoat style allows the activities to take over. It responds to the increased amount of leisure time available to young people by offering more and more entertainment to fill that time, rather than viewing leisure provision as a means of social education.

One of the central tasks of adolescence is the establishment of a sense of personal identity. Crucial to that identity is a job, since our society, whether we like or agree with it or not, remains one in which human identity, status and dignity are inextricably bound up with work. Psychologists have described how it is the consequences of work rather than work itself that meets human needs since they impose a structure, provide shared experiences and contacts, and enforce activity. No work means one less tool with which young people can achieve a sense of identity. The adult status attained by being in work is being denied to increasing numbers of young people and although there are a variety of routes to adulthood, becoming a parent for example, or finding a place of your own to live (the former being increasingly used to achieve the latter), having a job remains a major one. The redcoat style of youth work offers a level of experience that affords little opportunity for young people to begin to define for themselves their own identity, little opportunity for questioning their situation or for achieving adult role or status. The provision of the redcoat style is enjoyed by many and it has its place; but that place is outside the Youth Service.

Does this mean that youth work which has social education as its aim is therefore not concerned with leisure activities, enjoyment or fun? Of course not. Youth work incorporates all these but in addition responds to the need of young people to be of significance, to be listened to, to have a place of their own and to begin to achieve a sense of personal identity. Being listened to has been identified by young people as one of the things they most value about youth clubs (DES, 1983, p. 39). A youth club can offer an opportunity for young people to assume responsibility, share experiences and participate in decision-making. Doing these things can develop the ability to negotiate, plan, argue, gather information, work co-operatively, identify issues and make mistakes, all of which contribute towards establishing that sense of identity. In the face of the seemingly overwhelming odds that are stacked against young people today, there is a tendency to overlook or even dismiss the very real impact such youth work can make on their lives.

One of the underlying values of community work is 'to give practical expression in a great many different ways to a philosophy that puts people at the centre of things' (Calouste Gulbenkian Foundation, 1973, p. 16). Given that one of the stated aims of the Youth Service is the active participation of young people in the Service, then clearly this is a value underlying youth work as well. The leisure provision of the redcoat style of youth work puts people at the centre of things only to the extent that they are the consumers of such provision. It is youth work, not leisure provision that seeks to put young people at the centre of things in an active rather than a passive way.

The situation of young people today demands a Youth Service committed to empowering them to make and take their place in society. Such a service manifestly requires youth workers; redcoats will simply not do.

Acknowledgements

I am grateful to the following colleagues whose experience I have drawn on in compiling the practical examples given in this chapter: Roger Dibben, Surrey Youth and Community Service; Colin Grant, London Borough of Sutton Youth Service; Julie Janes, Surrey Youth and Community Service; John Turner, London Borough of Sutton Youth Service.

2

Youth Workers as Social Workers

BRUCE BRITTON

A recent survey found, rather unsurprisingly, that young people view youth clubs as somewhere to go where they can meet and make friends and enjoy themselves in a relaxed atmosphere (DES, 1983). Top of the youngsters' list of expectations of youth workers was not organisational ability, enthusiasm or activity skills, but willingness to focus on individuals, listen to their views and treat them as if they were capable of exercising responsibility.

Youth workers have traditionally responded to this expectation by making themselves 'approachable' to any young person who might want to talk. Sometimes this is not an adequate response, particularly when the individual's concerns are complex or involve other agencies, and it relies on vying for the attention of a small number of adults in a club full of people. At some point the youth worker may well be asked to move from a relatively 'neutral' counselling role to a more explicitly interventionist or advocacy role. Here it is the welfare of the individual which is primarily at stake rather than the general well-being of the young people in the club or neighbourhood. Different skills and knowledge are demanded and youth workers may well find themselves venturing into unfamiliar terrain better known to social workers. For some youth workers this might be a fairly exceptional if not uncomfortable experience; others may intentionally choose this near 'casework' approach because it appears to be the most effective way to provide a worthwhile service for some of the most disadvantaged young people in their neighbourhood.

This chapter will look at what it is like to be a youth worker operating as 'social worker'. Sections will focus on the problems, constraints and possibilities of working in this way, and the chapter concludes with an examination of the wider implications of using a 'social work' approach in a voluntary-sector youth work setting. Whilst the arguments refer to youth work in Scotland (which has its own unique system of organisation), many of the issues will be only too familiar to colleagues elsewhere. No apology is made for what may be seen as a somewhat partisan piece. The Scottish system is not without its weaknesses and the development of youth-related services in Scotland remains a subject for heated debate (Stead and Britton, 1984), yet the official systems for dealing with delinquent and 'problem' youth in Scotland are potentially more humane and constructive than their counterparts south of the Border. It is against this backdrop that community based youth projects have evolved.

Youth/social work in practice

There is a locally managed youth project based in a large local authority housing estate in Edinburgh. The project, called the Pilton Youth Programme (PYP), is funded jointly by local and central government but retains an 'independent' status as a voluntary organisation. It was originally set up as a result of local concern to keep truants off the streets, but during the thirteen years of its existence the aims of PYP have evolved to meet the changing needs of young people in its catchment area. Central to its purpose now is reducing the number of inappropriate residential placements of local youngsters aged between twelve and eighteen years by establishing services ranging from individual counselling through family work and small group work to more widely available youth clubs. The project adheres to a number of basic principles including non-stigmatised availability of services, diversion from statutory intervention, voluntary attendance, community involvement, minimal intervention, negotiation and participation. What these mean in practice will become apparent later. PYP forms part of a local network of support for young people focused on the welfare of individuals. The project is recognised by statutory agencies such as the Social Work and Education Departments and also the Children's Hearing System which is charged with the responsibility for making decisions about compulsory measures for the care or control of young people. The 'welfare' basis of Children's Hearings which set the context for the aims and methods of PYP (and a number of other youth projects in Scotland) is particularly amenable to the involvement of individuals, such as youth project workers, from outside the statutory sector.

The change from offering youth provision designed to keep kids off the streets to a much more individualised intervention-ist and welfare-orientated role arose largely out of the recognition that many young people who ended up in care or in a 'List D School' (the Scottish equivalent of a CHE) were little different from their peers. These young people, as a result of coming to the attention of the Social Work Department, Reporter to the Children's Panel or Education Welfare Department, set in motion a process which often developed its own momentum and logic and could ultimately result in their removal from home. Whilst conceding that this drastic action was necessary in certain limited cases, it was felt that the opportunities which already existed within the juvenile justice system to divert young people away from further statutory intervention could only logically be reinforced from outside the statutory sector. Since social workers, police and Reporters dealt with young people as individual 'cases', it was this rather than any belief in the intrinsic superiority of 'casework' over more conventional youth work practice which determined the decision to place much more emphasis on this approach.

When the process by which local youngsters ended up on home or residential supervision was investigated, it was found that the individualised approach to cases seemed to be reflected in the idiosyncratic procedures of the departments. In fact, until recently there was little or no consistent policy to guide social workers in their dealings with young people and as a result a 'better safe than sorry' approach had grown by default. This meant that many social workers saw it as too 'risky' to argue for keeping young petty offenders out of residential care when all other options had been exhausted. The argument ran that there they would at least be kept out of trouble. The unintended consequences of this approach meant that some of the young people from the estate who had perfectly adequate homes were being placed in residential care almost despite the explicit humanitarian aims of the Children's Hearing System. It was felt that the PYP project had a responsibility to intervene on behalf of and alongside these youngsters by encouraging the statutory agencies to make less intrusive but more 'risky' decisions. This could best be achieved by providing a voluntary alternative to statutory supervision so that fewer young people would be carried along by the momentum which ultimately led to the decision to remove them from their home and neighbourhood.

At the same time as providing an intensive service for individuals it was crucial to maintain a range of services available to any local young person. The reasons for this will be explored in greater depth later in the chapter. The strategy which evolved from this decision consisted of a balance of club-based youth work for any local young people in the twelve to sixteen years age range (the 'Open' group) and the provision of two 'Membership' groups each catering for a maximum of ten young people, who were also worked with individually. Although the groups were quite different in their aims, many of the methods used were common to both. Neither is new or revolutionary in its approach but both played an equally crucial role in achieving the project's aims and it was the interplay between both which provided the sound basis for effective and non-stigmatising individual work.

Problems and constraints

Focusing on individuals within youth work has its own inherent problems but when the setting for this approach is a voluntary project there are further complicating factors. Credibility, influence and the assumptions of users, neighbours and statutory agencies have to be established or resolved.

Building a sound interpersonal relationship with a young person may well be worthwhile in itself but is better seen as a means to an end within good youth work practice. The 'end' may be a resolution of a particular problem, such as helping someone negotiate a return to school after a period of suspension. To achieve this the youth worker must gain trust and credibility not only with the young person but also with the teacher, head teacher and, if one is involved, the social worker. For youth workers in a voluntary agency, credibility is often hard-won, particularly with colleagues in statutory agencies who may see them as 'mavericks', challenging their restrictive roles whilst appearing to have little or no accountability. Taking on an advocacy role or supporting young people in their dealings with the authorities often involves negotiating concessions from agencies which have statutory responsibilities and duties. From a position of relative powerlessness youth workers have to establish room to manoeuvre so that they can create space for the young person's views to be considered. Invariably, any space conceded arises from the external agency's assessment of the youth project's practice. In the PYP project it was decided to confront this issue directly by identifying key sites of decision-making about young people, such as the Reporter to the Children's Panel who has discretion to call or avoid a Hearing, and the Children's Panel which has discretion about the disposal made at a Hearing. The intention was to establish credibility with those responsible for making these crucial decisions. The provision of a tangible service as well as opinions about what was felt should happen to young people undoubtedly helped here. One of the main criticisms of moving towards a focused individual orientation in a youth work setting is the inevitability of individualising problems which are common to almost all young people in a neighbourhood. It is argued that this lays the foundations for a 'treatment' approach which only serves to reinforce, both within the individual and in the eyes of the community, the young person's personal maladjustment and inadequacy. More insidiously, it relegates the individual and his or her family, friends and neighbours to the role of passive consumers of whatever professional services are deemed necessary to treat their problems (Ward, 1982). In other words, by working exclusively with individuals, youth workers may be more likely to reinforce rather than challenge the worst undermining aspects of welfare provision.

It is in recognition of this that PYP has encouraged and developed the involvement of local adults and young people in the management and running of the project, particularly in the 'Open' group referred to earlier. This policy has done a great deal to ensure that the project has secure roots in the neighbourhood and is not seen either as a 'sin bin' for delinquents who are excluded from other youth facilities, or as an extension to currently existing social service provision.

A further criticism often levelled at projects which work on similar lines is that they can unintentionally accelerate the momentum with which 'problem' youngsters are involved with the authorities. Whilst this criticism is often justified within the English system, the same is not necessarily true in Scotland, where the juvenile justice system operates on different principles. PYP representatives have often attended Children's Hearings with young people who are already involved with the project and for whom new grounds for appearance have arisen such as truanting, solvent abuse or offences. Provided the Panel members have been satisfied with the PYP workers' proposal, the youngsters have invariably been allowed to remain involved with the project rather than be made the subject of more intrusive disposals such as home or residential supervision. In such cases PYP workers have argued repeatedly and successfully that on the basis of the young person's needs, statutory intervention would still be over-hasty and inappropriate.

Clearly this level of influence over decisions concerning young people carries with it a considerable degree of responsibility. In dealings with the Children's Hearing System on behalf of youngsters who attend PYP the workers are acutely aware that they participate in Hearings as invited 'friends' of the young people and not by virtue of their status as youth workers. Once involved with an individual it is felt that he or she has a 'right' to continued support and representation by the project.

Whether justified or not, in terms of help statutory social services are perceived as the 'end of the line' by many people and it is not difficult to understand why. Most people have friends or relatives to whom they can turn at times of crisis. It is usually only when these sources of help or support have been tried unsuccessfully that 'the welfare' is approached. People are often discouraged by their dealings with social workers because the agency tends to redefine requests for help in a demeaning way. The request for help about one problem may well be used to justify prying into other areas which are, quite reasonably, considered private by the client. Even the terminology of social work reinforces this one-sided power relationship. Many adults would rather go without professional help because they are unwilling to put up with such an intrusion. Some young people also view statutory social work in the same way. Hill, writing about a youth counselling service, describes how many young people have said to her, 'I didn't think I was bad enough to go to social services' (1979, p. 10). PYP guards against making an intrusion on the privacy of individuals as the price they have to pay for help, advice or support.

Working effectively with individuals, particularly in their dealings with other agencies, can be extremely time-consuming as it can involve the joint preparation of reports and letters, and attendance at 'case' reviews, interviews or meetings concerning and including the individual. This has obvious implications for the amount of work which can be carried by youth workers using this approach. PYP operates a key worker system where each member of the project staff takes responsibility for all the individual, family and liaison work concerning a particular young person. Each staff member would rarely act as key worker for more than five individuals, each of whom would also be attending a Membership group. The key workers also share responsibility for wider administrative and organisational aspects of the project and for work with other individuals who seek the project's help either through informal contact or by attending the 'Open' group.

The core of the work is the face-to-face contact either individually through counselling, with the young person at home in their family, or at a PYP group. Each of these three elements is potentially as important as the others and each requires specific skills. For those with a youth work or community work background the family work can often seem particularly threatening, though workers with a training in social work may well be more confident in this area but less so with group- or club-based work. At PYP this potential constraint to the project's development was overcome both through staff recruitment and clear policies about the way the project should operate. Maintaining a balance of approaches to youth work is difficult and it can be easy for staff members to become so involved with individuals that the groupwork or the wider principles of the project, such as participation and collective action, can be submerged. If this happens, the experience for the youngster can quickly change from feeling supported by the project to feeling stifled or controlled. The net result of this would be an extension of the powerlessness they endure in their dealings with other agencies, and PYP would become virtually indistinguishable from the authorities whose approach can be so restrictive.

Powerlessness is not restricted to the young people who use the project. PYP's status as a voluntary organisation, particularly in dealings with local authority departments, often made the workers feel like David to the local authority's Goliath, but the smallness of stature also gave improved manoeuvrability. Crossing the traditional departmental boundaries of youth work and social work raises many issues concerning funding and evaluation. The grants for PYP are currently shared between central government and the Social Work and Education Departments of the local authority (in Scotland the Education Department has responsibility for youth services through Community Education). Each has its own priorities and criteria for evaluating success. None of these neatly fits the policy and practice of youth/social work at PYP and this can create problems of categorisation, particularly for those who have to make decisions about the project's future funding. Is PYP a glorified youth club and hence part of youth work, or a diluted adolescent unit which is better seen as a corollary of social work? Vulnerability is currently a price which has to be paid for the independence which can allow creative and relevant work with young people. Some of the possibilities contained in this approach are explored in the next section.

Possibilities

Perhaps the most exciting possibility to arise from transferring a 'social work' approach to youth work practice is the opportunity to shake off the self-imposed constraints and misconceptirons of particular work disciplines. The 'tunnel vision' which gives rise to these constraints often flows from a lack of mutual understanding of the role of youth worker and social worker. Social workers are frequently viewed with suspicion by youth workers, who may see them as agents of social control charged with considerable legal power to intervene in the lives of young people. Social workers usually become involved with young people at a time of crisis and often as a result of parental neglect, juvenile offending or truancy. Youth workers, therefore, tend to equate social workers with statutory duties which are discharged through the Children's Hearings or Juvenile Court. The corollary of this is that youth workers are inclined to view any issues which have a statutory component as the exclusive domain of the social worker. This undoubtedly has its origins in the training each profession receives but it is reinforced on a day-to-day basis by the adopted procedures in local authority departments.

If youth workers frequently see social workers as 'soft policemen' who have a distorted view of youth because they only come into contact with young people when they are facing problems, then many social workers seem to view youth workers with a mixture of disdain or condescension tinged with envy. The disdain arises from the youth workers' apparent lack of statutory responsibilities and the envy occurs for perhaps the same reason.

Although this is a somewhat superficial account of the mutual lack of regard and understanding which can arise between workers, it has a serious side. Firstly, mutual suspicion between workers is not conductive to co-operation or the sharing of methods and approaches. Secondly, social workers may by virtue of their statutory authority effectively exclude youth workers from participating in any important discussions about young people. In both cases, those who suffer most are the young people themselves, whose future can depend on the outcome of a particularly significant decision made by, or on the recommendation of, a social worker. Moreover, the social worker may have had only a brief contact with the individual concerned. Youth workers often know the young people in their neighbourhood through their attendance at a youth club.

They may have extensive knowledge of a particular individual's circumstances and be aware of many positive aspects of his or her behaviour and character. Unless they are aware of an impending appearance at a Children's Hearing or court and unless they are prepared (or allowed) to disclose this information to the officials concerned, their assessment obviously cannot be taken into consideration. In such cases, counselling based at a youth centre may be of some value to the young person with its emphasis on non-directiveness, but it is unlikely to meet his or her immediate need for active support, advice and advocacy. The more interventionist stance advocated in this chapter has the advantage of pursuing, whenever necessary, the person-centred and problem-focused approach of social work but in a context which is free from the organisational constraints and statutory basis of local authority social work. It is casework by consent and is based on clear aims and objectives agreed by both parties and open to regular review and evaluation.

Workers carrying out focused work with individuals from outside the statutory sector are in a unique position. They are immediately made aware of the power which statutory organisations have over the destinies of young people, but unlike the local authority departments which have to discharge legal responsibilities they have potentially less vested interest in the way things are.

Youth workers in this position not only have the opportunity but also, arguably, the responsibility to bring about a change in the policy and practice which dictate the way young people are dealt with if they create problems. There are also various organisational possibilities for change. Youth workers can generalise their experience of tackling issues with particular young people and identify areas where statutory agencies can be brought together to develop local policies for youth. By example, youth workers can encourage statutory agencies to abandon the 'fail safe' approach to decision-making which increases the likelihood of further statutory intervention at a later stage and thereby develop the practice as well as the principle of minimal intervention. By reinterpreting behaviour or simply by showing another aspect of the young people's lives, youth workers can redress the balance of opinion about young people who might be seen only in terms of their delinquency or disruptive behaviour. Finally, if it becomes necessary to remove young people from their homes, the youth worker can maintain contact with them and help plan for an earlier supported return home than might otherwise be possible.

These are all possibilities which have been put into practice at PYP and have benefited not only those young people with whom it has worked directly but others also, through the 'knock-on' effects of policy change and practical support.

Conclusion

This chapter began by referring to young people's desire to be seen as responsible individuals who should be allowed more control over their lives. The policies and practices of local authority departments allow for only very limited participation by young people in what are often critical decisions about their future. As a result, many youngsters view the decisions made about them as arbitrary or unfair. When matters reach crisis point it often seems that those most in need of support and help are 'sacrificed' by youth workers who are more often concerned with the welfare of the majority, not least because the individuals are seen as either too demanding or too disruptive to be contained in large groups or clubs. Ultimately, the interests of these youngsters have been left to social workers who receive referrals usually because the youngsters have come to the attention of school guidance staff, the police or the Reporter as a result of their behaviour. The social services frequently seem to lose sight of an individual's needs and pursue a predetermined course which may not only have harmful, unintended consequences for the youngster but may even result in decisions which are inconsistent with the department's own aims.

PYP responded to this dilemma by positively discriminating in favour of those young people who required support in their dealings with the authorities and by combining social work and youth work methods to provide a flexible, imaginative and accessible service. The strategy which has evolved at PYP is not without its problems and constraints but avoids some of the more undermining experiences of local authority social work provision. By maintaining close links with adults and young people in the neighbourhood and encouraging their involvement in both the youth work practice and the management of the project PYP reinforced its standing and credibility as an organisation. Young people and their parents will turn to PYP for help or advice because they feel they have a stake in the way the project operates. It is 'their' project in a tangible and personal way which could never be said about the local authority Social Work Department.

The practice and procedures which have been evolved at PYP arise from an understanding of the problems experienced by local young people and not from preconceived departmental responsibilities, methods or theoretical foundations. This has allowed the combination of different approaches, which may at first seem incompatible, into a model of practice which is consistent with the principles of juvenile justice and welfare in Scotland. The model has become increasingly influential, not only in local social work and youth work practice but also in departmental policy making within local authorities through the development of regional youth social work strategies. More recently regional youth work policies have begun to reflect the aims and priorities of youth projects such as PYP and provide tangible evidence of the impact that innovative youth work practice can have on policy-making (Strathclyde Regional Council, 1984). Indeed, far from becoming detached from organisational issues, a commitment to focused work with individuals helped the youth/social workers at PYP to clarify their role and that of other workers in the field.

An example of this 'knock-on' effect was the establishment in area of a monitoring group consisting of PYP staff and social workers. The purpose of this group was to ensure that all community alternatives were fully explored before compulsory supervision was considered for young people who were about to attend Children's Hearings. In this way, PYP staff were in a position to help divert young people away from unnecessary or over-hasty compulsory measures.

This co-operation has arisen as a result of proving PYP's

approach in practice. It is maintained by a sustained dialogue with managers and practitioners in Social Work and Education Departments and is favourably viewed by Reporter and Panel members alike within the Children's Hearing System.

The final and most important measure of the success of this youth/social work approach is the impact it has on the lives of particular individuals. Almost two-thirds of the young people who came to PYP for specific help in the three years up to 1984 were successfully diverted from compulsory measures of care at Children's Hearings (PYP, 1984, p. 24).

Whilst it is not possible to be certain, the workers at PYP had every reason to believe that the majority of these youngsters would otherwise have been subject to residential supervision without the specific intervention of the project. This more than anything else is confirmation that focused individual work as part of a wider overall strategy can be a worthwhile and effective element of good youth work practice.

3

Youth Workers as Community Workers

FRAN LACEY

Community work and youth work are not synonymous in either practice or definition. There are important differences. However, there does seem to me to be an increasingly large area of work where mutual learning and co-operation would be of enormous benefit both to workers, and perhaps more importantly, to those people in whose interest youth workers and community workers are employed. There are, of course, a number of projects where this mutuality has been recognised and for the most part these have been neighbourhood youth work projects. It appears that the reason the value of this linkage has not been more commonly acknowledged lies in the workers' experience of language and hence the boundaries they construct around their work. The possibility of confusion in roles occurs when one moves outside the simple associations of youth work with youth, and community work with the community, meaning adults.

In this chapter, it is intended to have a brief look at the history of community work and youth work in order to shed some light on the relationship between the two. Some 'typical' youth work scenarios will be examined and it will be considered whether there are aspects of the task, method and philosophy that could be helpfully redefined if youth workers are seen as community workers. Finally, some of the very real issues and dilemmas that can emerge from the implementation of a community development approach to youth work will be examined.

The Fairbairn–Milson Report officially recommended that:

> A Youth and Community Service should be established which will get away from the club-is-the-youth-service approach, meet the needs of young people by making contact with them *wherever* they are to be found, and recognise them as part of the community. (DES, 1969, p. 1, emphasis as in original)

The report also recommended the expansion of school-based youth work and the development of the use of schools by the wider community. It stressed that the Youth and Community Service must recognise the adult status of those clients drawn from the upper age range who 'must be encouraged to play an active part in a society in which they themselves will help to mould' (Ibid. p. 2). These and other recommendations indicate a desire to break down the separation of work with young people from work with the rest of the community, although there were no explicit recommendations that community work methods would also be appropriate for work with young people. While a report like this can provide a tremendous amount of encouragement and can promote real progress in a certain direction, there is always a danger that it is seen as being more innovatory than it really is. There had certainly been neighbourhood youth work in existence for many years prior to 1969. As Kuenstler (1955) shows in his discussion of 'spontaneous youth groups', which exist on or well beyond the periphery of the Youth Service and have been a common feature of city life throughout the years.

The recent history of much community work has led to a view in certain sectors that youth workers as community workers may be a dangerous idea. For community work has acquired a culture or reputation for challenging the status quo and being engaged in politics and the allocation of resources. Youth work, on the other hand, has retained a more conservative image, although in the last few years, there has been an increasing challenge to the 'traditional' youth work model, spearheaded primarily by women and black workers confronting sexist and racist styles of work. However, those youth workers who are not principally involved in running a building-based programme are more easily linked with the community, and therefore the notion of them as community workers, and the acknowledgement of a common purpose may occur. Where it does, the sharing of skills and methods may also be more readily accepted by the workers, although the youth work authorities may be concerned by the implications.

One of the attractive challenges of the concept of youth workers having something in common with community work, and at times doing community work or using community work methods, is the potential for 'unlocking the building'. This would free the energy and resources of young people, workers and associated adults which can be re-directed towards 'helping people to influence the distribution of resources . . . as a way of promoting political responsibility and communal coherence' (Thomas, 1983, p. 112).

Consequently, the focus on young people as the legitimate prime interest group for youth workers can be justified either on the grounds that they are an integral part of the community, when the community is defined as a locality, or that they constitute a 'community of interest', that is, a separate group who are often neglected or even at times deliberately excluded, in the interests of adults. The important point is that this distinction between youth and community does not exist or is not as valid as it might at first appear. Take, for example, any one of a number of large, full-time youth clubs or centres, then three characteristics would be common to them all:

1. A significant proportion of the regular users will come from one or two estates or neighbourhoods.
2. There will be a number of adults working there on a voluntary or part-time basis who may well have come up 'through the ranks' or live in the same community as the members.
3. The full-time worker will spend time working with these adults in staff meetings, supervision sessions or informal chats.

Given that these characteristics are fairly common, then one of the often quoted differences between youth workers and community workers, and one of the arguments used against neighbourhood youth work, namely that youth workers work with young people and community workers work with adults, is shown to be a misconception. One of the reasons why this misconception is maintained is the process by which adults and young people who work in a club become 'staff'. Working with adults is renamed staff supervision, support or coping with staff problems. This process also has its effect on the staff, for in the process of becoming staff, they are to an extent divested of the richness of their life's experiences: including their awareness and knowledge of, views about and involvement in, the community in which they live. If community is taken to mean not only the geographical community, but also one based perhaps on race, gender, employment or unemployment, then the potential for community development, community action or social planning, using the life experiences, knowledge and skills of the adults alongside those of the young people, becomes clearer:

> All of us have picked up . . . biographical luggage. We are bound to call upon this to a greater or lesser degree. The worry remains that unless what we call 'experience' is identified, discussed and selectively reinforced through training two things happen. First, experiences may wither for lack of 'exercise'. Secondly, experiences which may not be desirable can remain unchanged. (Bolger and Scott, 1984, p. 27)

In suggesting that youth club workers could refocus their work with adults in this way, it is also suggested that these skills and experience are seen as legitimate 'luggage' to bring to youth work and legitimate areas in which to involve oneself as a worker with young people. There is a real potential for young people to become involved in community activities and campaigns, and for young people to begin to organise activities for themselves around their own interests. There is, and will always be, scope for youth clubs in the sense of a building given over for significant portions of time to the activities of young people and a refocusing of the time and energy spent by both young people and adults (staff) towards some of the tasks and areas of concern more commonly attributed to community work. This would be an exciting and stimulating prospect – one that is entirely in keeping with Youth Service rhetoric around social and political education and participation.

In the above discussion, one of the issues highlighted was the degree to which building-based youth work did, in fact, involve the full-time youth worker in some of the activities which have been argued as differentiating community workers from youth workers. For some building-based youth workers the amount of time and energy they spend working with adults from the local community is all too painfully real to them. What is referred to in this chapter is the experience of some youth workers who are responsible for the smooth running of a programme of activities in a centre which, either for financial or philosophical reasons, is used by a number of other community groups. For some workers, this means that a vast amount of their time is caught up in arbitrating between different groups, collecting money, making sure the rooms are ready, answering an endless stream of 'Could I just ask you . . .' questions, and so on. Each one of these may, in itself, be a valid use of time, but together they amount to a disproportionate input to running the centre for community rather than youth work. It is suggested that the root cause of situations like this lies not in the incompatibility of the community using a youth club building, for if young people are not using the building then allowing other groups in the area to rent space is a positive use of resources, with potential for spin-offs into work with and by young people. The problem lies rather in the lack of clarity around the role of the worker and the appropriateness of their responsibilities for administrating a building. So long as the youth worker is seen to be singularly in control of the centre and available, then it is inevitable that a group coming in to run a session will turn to him or her for whatever help is needed. For example, a mothers' and toddlers' group that finds cigarette ends all over the floor and the fireguard removed is going to want some immediate response. They are going to be angry, and want someone to hear and acknowledge that anger. They are going to want an explanation and reassurance that it won't happen again. They will need to know where the guard is to make the fire safe, or what is available as an alternative. They may want someone else to clear up before they let the toddlers loose to chew the cigarette ends, or pull them gleefully apart. Who is responsible for the room being in that state, or as it is more often seen, who is the guilty party, is a question that can be, and often is, debated for hours or days, or agreed in two minutes flat. The point is that this situation, in whatever guise it arises, requires time and energy. While each situation is dealt with individually, the frustration around the amount of time spent in running the centre is bound to build up in a youth worker. This reflects two assumptions: firstly, that work with young people is about face-to-face interventions involving either leisure activities, counselling or informal chats. Secondly, that running a centre is an administrative job that requires a degree in public relations.

However, if youth workers take on, albeit briefly, the cloak of community workers, they will then be able to reduce these frustrations and see their responsibilities in running the centre in a different way. In practice, this means youth workers encouraging young people to become more involved in the running of the centre. The following are some ideas about how this involvement could take place. For example, many of the decisions made by full-time workers (or the managers of a centre) are informed by knowledge of the finances. While this information is often given piecemeal to young people by way of explanation in a particular situation, (usually concerning a shortage of money), there is rarely a systematic and effective attempt to educate regular users of centres in matters of overall finances. If such an attempt were made, then the young people would be in a position to understand fully the way in which the centre was managed and why, in the instance of a shortage of cash, it was necessary to have other groups using the centre. This is distinctly different from young people feeling they have been 'fobbed off' with the usual adult excuse of 'no money'. Young people, when they have been given the opportunity to understand the rationale and facts, are likely to co-operate rather than be obstuctive. This example may be taken further when young people are empowered to make or influence decisions concerning the management of the centre. Their active involvement in ensuring that decisions are implemented is then likely to be greater.

Similarly, young people can play an active part in the running of the centre. This can be done during the day if they are unemployed, or out of school or work hours. The important aspect of this approach is to ensure that the young people are given the responsibility of the job, not asked merely to 'help out' or 'run errands' for the full-time worker, which is often the message given. The ways in which this is organised, on either a regular paid or voluntary basis, may vary with the work being done. The areas of responsibility which could be taken on by more young people are numerous. Here are a few suggestions:

1. Staffing the office for blocks of time and taking responsibility for dealing with as many of the personal callers and telephone calls as possible, referring-on those that require the attention of the full-time worker. This would include responding to complaints from user groups.
2. Opening up the building to user groups. This may need to be checked in terms of the safety of the young person involved, bearing in mind that there may be individuals or groups who wish to take advantage in an abusive way of the building or resources.
3. Canteen, cafeteria or tuck shop work which involves checking and buying stock, being responsible for the money and accounts, and serving customers, can be passed over in part or entirely to young people. It could, indeed, be suggested as a small enterprise for two or three young unemployed people so they would be responsible for and benefit from any income they could derive from it.
4. Receiving, welcoming and playing 'host' to the number of visitors who want to see round the building, explaining what goes on and introducing the people who use it.
5. Taking responsibility for the booking of rooms, equipment, minibuses or tutors.
6. Responsibility for checking equipment, ensuring its maintenance and showing others how to use it. This could involve office equipment such as a duplicator or photocopier, or items such as videos and pool tables.
7. Liaison with user groups.
8. Production of annual general reports.
9. The organisation of particular fund-raising events.
10. Administrative and office work, from filing and typing to maintaining notice boards and circulating relevant publications to staff and volunteers (such as training news, periodicals and articles).

11. Running a creche; and
12. Producing a newsletter.

It is not suggesting that young people's involvement in any or all of these areas would be problem-free, or that the youth worker could simply hand over the jobs and forget about them. Youth workers are invited to shift the emphasis of their work towards enabling young people and, where appropriate, other members of the community, to take on the work and responsibilities involved in the running of the centre.

This discussion has been focused on looking at ways in which youth work can develop towards a style of work more usually associated with community work. However, the discussion has mostly engaged with issues concerning building-based workers. In the context of non-building-based youth work, it is usually assumed that workers have already developed their practice along community-work lines. This assumption is based on a belief that their work is in the community rather than in youth clubs. In the same way that youth work in clubs and centres can be developed along community work lines, so there is a similar choice when it comes to non-club-based work.

This final section will examine in more detail youth work as community work out in the community. Much of this will be based on experience of neighbourhood youth work in a project based at a settlement. The process of setting up and developing the project highlighted three significant aspects of youth work as community work.

The first point is that the establishment of the need for, and the type of, provision was achieved through working within the community and gathering information. The origins of this particular project lay in work on playschemes, which in turn emphasised the need for provision year-round and the potential for local residents to be involved using the community halls on the estates. Further information was collected using survey methods, including interviews with tenants' groups and young people, and information from the local authority.

Secondly, there was a need for the shift in method and philosophy from 'providing' to 'enabling' to be clearly structured into the project, and therefore into the workers' job descriptions. Without this, the worker would have been vulnerable to pressures to supply youth provision and would have had no mandate to engage in the process of community development. After the first six months, it became clear that the job descriptions were not specific enough in the mandate that they gave the workers, and they were amended to ensure that the primary task was working with local residents to enable them to enhance the skills necessary for the development of club or similar youth provision.

The third aspect was the acknowledgement of the process by which an agency becomes involved with a community. To respond to initiatives from the community means that there must be a basic structure of organisation within the community, a commitment by the residents and a knowledge of who and how to ask for help. While these prerequisites existed in this project, there are many communities where they do not, for a host of reasons. If a project remains purely responsive it may mean that provision for young people does not materialise. On the other hand, consistent with the community work approach are a number of other options that a youth project can take. Thomas (1983) argues that community work is a combination of five approaches which, although having their own tasks, methods and outcomes, all lead to a greater political responsibility and 'communal coherence'. One such approach he describes as social planning, which comprises:

> . . . the analysis of social conditions, social policies and agency services, the setting of goals, and priorities, the design of service programmes and the mobilisation of appropriate resources, and the implementation and evaluation of services and programmes. (p. 109)

In practice this might mean a youth worker assessing needs and problems and the community's own strengths and resources, establishing which estates or areas currently lacked youth provision and were not making demands, then planning appropriate strategies so that the needs of young people in the area could be met. In the short term, this might mean a consortium of workers such as Education Welfare Officers, social workers, youth workers and play workers running a summer scheme to increase morale and generate new interest and enthusiasm in order to make new contacts. It may mean supporting an existing tenants' association in asking for a youth worker to be allocated; or encouraging more systematic research regarding the young people, what they want and what can realistically be achieved. In the long term this could result in a full-time youth worker being allocated to the estate on a permanent basis to do detached work; or a new project set up to work within a particular area of concern, such as drug misuse. Equally, managers of existing provision might be encouraged to change their policy to allow use by the young people in the area, or to meet the needs of a particular group such as girls and young women. It may eventually result in the residents, whether young people or adults, organising their own provision.

Maintaining a community work approach does not rule out the possibility of direct provision for young people by the worker or project. That may be the appropriate outcome at a particular point in time. The significant difference is the process of social planning and community assessment and involvement that occurs, and the options that are considered in deciding how best to proceed.

One of the exciting developments that happened as a result of this continuous approach to youth work in the locality of the project over a number of years was the 'normalising' of the idea of running your own provision. This acceptance that it was achievable became sufficiently strong that the young people themselves became actively involved. The process varied. On one estate, the young people gradually took over as managers of clubs and projects as the interest of the adults dwindled. On another, a group of young people who had attended a youth club on the estate run by adults, which had closed, decided that they wanted to re-open it for themselves. On a third estate young people started from scratch. Amongst other groups, adults and young people worked together to run the club. The immediacy of the locally-based provision and the confidence derived from seeing the people they knew doing the work of manager and youth workers was tremendously important in understanding the readiness of young people to take on the responsibility.

It is significant, however, that in the early days of the project the adults were less able to accept this situation. On one estate the election of an 18-year-old as chairperson of the youth club management committee caused such anxiety that the chair of the tenants' association demanded the keys to the hall, asserting that no 'child' could possibly be responsible for opening and shutting. On the same estate, the youth club has now been run almost entirely by 'children' aged 15 to 20 for some three to four years, with just one adult as treasurer. Whether the young people organise the provision for themselves alone, or for themselves and others, and whether this is seen as part of the community facilities and community structures and supported by adults, depends on the history and culture of the areas, as much as on the young people themselves.

This chapter so far has implied that communities on estates or in a particular area are homogeneous, and therefore by using a community work approach an area or estate can acquire some of the necessary resources for its young people. This is obviously far from the truth. If community work is 'associated with a particular kind of critique of existing arrangements of power and resources' (Thomas, 1983, p. 118), then youth workers who adopt this style of work must be aware of the need for this 'critique' within the estate, as well as in the wider context.

A group of adults or young people who wish to set up some kind of youth provision in a tenants' hall, say, are likely to face obstruction and insensitivity. For many groups it is a continual battle where the youth club is made a scapegoat and blamed for noise and damage on the estate seven nights a week, even if it is only open on two. Often community halls with licensed bars set up self-perpetuating cycles whereby the cost of maintaining the bar and staff require that the bar is open Friday, Saturday and Sunday evenings, and two nights in the week, hence precluding weekend or extensive midweek use of the hall by youth groups, who do not generate profits.

At times, this constant struggle to assert the rights and needs of young people and their access to resources and facilities within their own communities seems to be a thankless waste of time and energy to all concerned. Young people, local adults who care about them and paid workers have all, at various times, decided that it is a process they no longer wish to put energy into and they have either settled for less than was wanted or needed, or gone elsewhere. Whether or not the final objective for individuals or groups is achieved, or if achieved, maintained, is not the sole consideration. Rather, it is equally important to recognise the benefits accruing from the growth in adult awareness of young people's needs, and in the skills and confidence that can be gained by both adults and young people from the process of securing resources.

Where groups do come together within communities to organise around the interests of young people, the question must be asked, 'Which young people's interests?'; also who is defining what these are and how they can best be met. So the 'critique of existing arrangements of power and resources' must extend to evaluating the relative power and access to resources of young men and women of different racial groups and how much say, if any, that disabled young people may have in the quality and style of youth provision. In looking at the significance of this for a community work approach to youth work, the following examples are indicative of the challenges posed.

A group of girls and young women were complaining that the youth club run by local adults was boring. After some discussion, encouraged by the project's workers, they approached the adults to ask for an extra night when they could pursue their interests. The adults, and particularly two of the women on the committee, were sympathetic and agreed to ask for an extra night. After much discussion, one night a month was agreed, on the basis that the girls' interests were not compatible with the club programme. The possibility of altering the main club programme was rejected. What was even more invidious was the subsequent pressure that was put on the girls' night to remain purely as a cooking and sewing session with occasional activities such as dance or self defence. As the hall was in the middle of the estate and had windows along two sides of it, any straying from cooking and sewing to playing pool or table tennis, or even occasionally talking, was remarked on and used as evidence by the boys and men on the committee that a girls' night was not needed. Over a period of time the existence of a girls' night for whatever the young women chose was asserted and became club policy. Yet three years later, when the tenants' association was complaining about the youth club, the vexed question was raised again of whether or not the girls' night was for sewing and cooking.

An underlying issue is the balance between educating those who are in control of resources within the community and ensuring that those who need and want the resources have access to them. It is no good assuming that the education can and will follow. If the girls and young women had been urged by the project workers to wait until the managers understood the need for girls-only provision, it is debatable whether the managers would have been able to convince those who controlled the hall. Anti-sexist and anti-racist youth work can be frustrated by the control of resources by such oppressive groups.

In another example, a tenants' association had campaigned to have a community hall built and were closely involved with planning the building. The building and programme reflected the interests and needs of the all-white tenants' association. The older generation of black adults became alienated from the tenants' association and the hall but the younger generation of black residents became interested in the youth provision and gradually both the club and the unemployed group became predominantly Afro-Caribbean. This caused considerable tension with the tenants' association who closed the hall on numerous occasions for spurious reasons, frequently complaining that the membership was not 'mixed' and that the workers 'discriminated' against the white young people. The anger and frustration this built up in the club's membership was acute and in turn led to petty damage to the building and apathy in terms of continuing to be involved in running the groups. The white tenants' association used this to vindicate their behaviour and actions. In recognising the issue of racism within white community groups, the project developed three strategies: to continue to support the black groups and individuals in asserting their rights; to raise the issue with the appropriate local authority departments who, in effect, controlled the resources; and to initiate racism awareness work with the white groups in conjunction with community workers where appropriate.

These two examples highlight the implications of working to

redress inequalities of power and opportunity within systems which are themselves inherently racist and sexist. In attempting to bring about changes in attitude and the balance of power and control, questions are raised as to how to work on both fronts, or whether to work on both fronts simultaneously. These become very real and dynamic issues.

The incorporating of community work strategies and techniques into youth work is clearly not without difficulties. However, the difficulties arise because, at a very real level, this style of youth work highlights and confronts the existing arrangements of power and resources. On some occasions the development of the work is thwarted by these existing arrangements. On many others it is part of the process of challenging and changing these arrangements and that is its vitality and justification.

The implication for workers is that it provides them with a structure for work which enables them to recognise and respond to expressed and unvoiced needs. Whether the process involves survey methods, dialogue with community groups or periods of work alongside people in the community, community approaches and ways of thinking can be creative: a way of developing a youth work practice that is appropriate to the needs and expectations of the particular groups of young people. Furthermore, the workers are involved in the potentially liberating process of enabling and not merely providing. This affects how they see their practice, and the young people and the communities with whom they work. In turn, this can and does allow the young people also to move out of the role of consumers and into a role which potentially acknowledges their creativity, responsibilities, power and adulthood.

4

Youth Workers as Educators

BILL ROSSETER

First and foremost, youth workers are educators. All other roles they may fulfil at certain times are secondary. The essential nature of their work is concerned with bringing about change. It is about moving young people on in some way from point A, not necessarily to point B or C, but to some position beyond point A. It is about the development within people of knowledge, skills and feelings. It is this emphasis located within the work that delineates the educator role from all the others.

Whatever emphasis workers may place on the benefits and gains to individuals, others may see education as fulfilling another role. Policy-makers and politicians, for example, may see education as a means of maintaining the status quo; a hierarchical social and economic order in which resources and power are unequally shared. For this reason, youth workers, depending on their individual motivations and beliefs and those of their employers may move young people on for a variety of reasons: to socialise them into a particular position within society; to improve their standing within society; to enable them to gain for themselves the resources necessary to analyse, criticise, challenge and change society itself.

Open and closed styles

Within education there are teachers – those who educate, and learners – those who are being educated. An established view of education says a number of things about them. Firstly, teachers are placed at a higher level than learners. They possess the knowledge, skills and feelings required by the learners. This they pour like liquid into the empty vessel heads of the learners. Acquiring this knowledge is the end product of learning, and great emphasis is placed on end products. Knowledge is owned by the teacher and it is their private property until they choose the time to give it away. It is compartmentalised and arranged hierarchically through a relatively rigid structure called the curriculum. Its content and rate on release is carefully controlled by them. There is emphasis on analytical, intellectual, linear thinking and primary reliance of theoretical and abstract knowledge. It is bureaucratically determined, almost totally resistant to community input or control. Learning is a one-way process from teacher to student.

The only active part played by learners is that they are expected to collect and soak up that which is poured in. If they do not do so they are clearly at fault. This style of education is concerned with developing normative behaviour. Those who reject it in whole or part are thought of, labelled and referred to, as problems. The hidden curriculum within this style is to teach that knowledge is private property and that to own it one only has to work hard. That those who possess greater amounts of it have higher authority and deserve respect and that it is necessary to submit meekly to this higher authority in order to gain reward. This is the closed style of education.

An alternative view looks at things rather differently. There are still teachers and learners but the one is not thought of as higher than the other. Indeed, the roles are interchangeable, the teacher learning at times, the learner teaching at times. Each recognises the other as possessing knowledge, skills and feelings and each values the other's experience. The relationship between the teacher and learner is formed on a basis of equality, trust and mutual respect. Teachers and learners are encouraged to see each other as people rather than as roles; sometimes even as friends. Within this style there is no fixed body of knowledge necessary to be passed on. Learning begins with that which immediately confronts the learner. It is not imposed externally through a curriculum. There is encouragement for divergent and creative thinking and a general striving for whole-person education. Emphasis is placed on discovering and learning things by experiencing them. Community involvement and control is positively encouraged. This is the open style of education.

Continual dialogue between teacher and learner ensures that both play an active part in the process. The world begins to be understood by confronting the problems faced by the learner. By posing questions the learner can answer, the problem may be overcome. The hidden curriculum of this style teaches that people should be valued for who they are rather than what they are, that everyone has something of value to offer others, that co-operation is more positive than conflict, that learning is a journey rather than a destination.

Attitudes, values and beliefs

It is unlikely that either the open or closed styles are used in their pure form. A range of factors will have influence over workers as to whether they are more open or more closed. Aims of the agency, settings for the work and the attitudes, values and beliefs of the workers are all likely to have an effect. Workers in some of the uniformed organisations are likely to tend to the closed style where discipline, obedience and respect for authority are the values they are likely to have themselves and would wish to be absorbed by those they work with.

This absorption is likely to occur, for learning is both a conscious and an unconscious process. It is important for workers to realise that in teaching knowledge and skills, how and what things are, ways of overcoming problems or difficulties, they are also teaching values. With the young people they are in contact with, the workers, by their own characters, can inspire honesty, co-operation, altruism, optimism, care and concern for others; or dishonesty, hypocrisy, pessimism, put-downs and competitiveness. For this reason the self-awareness of workers is very important. Youth workers need to check out how they come across to others. To recognise their own values and beliefs, to be open about them and realise the effect that they might have on others. Finally, they need to be open and committed to the concept of personal change.

Settings

As suggested already, settings also have an effect of shaping the style adopted, to a lesser or greater degree. Naturally open workers often have to change to a more closed style as a means of fitting in with the setting and its surrounding philosophy. Workers based on school sites are an example of this. The overall philosophy of the school may well demand more of a closed style than that required by the youth wing or centre. Because the overall control of the site is likely to be held by the head of the school, workers in this situation are likely to be forced to compromise. In all cases where work takes place within a building for which the worker has responsibility there are likely to be restrictions on adopting a purely open style.

For the detached worker this is not the case. They work where the young people are, in such places as shopping precincts and centres, cafés, public houses and amusement arcades. Not all young people congregate within such traditional detached-work settings. For many young women, disabled young people, arrivals in new towns and cities and young people with mental illness, for example, specific forms of detached or outreach provision need to be developed. Working with small groups or individuals in their homes, visiting all those new to a town or city with information about the area, visiting and befriending young people in hospitals, penal and other institutions are just some examples. The detached or outreach setting is perhaps ideal for those workers wishing to adopt an open style. The starting point is on the young person's territory and on their terms for any educative relationship that might ensue. If this is not understood by workers the young people can, and frequently do, turn their backs on them.

The range of building-based settings can be considerable. Because of the voluntary nature of the relationships between young people and youth workers, settings should be attractive and meet needs. If they fulfil neither of these criteria young people will not go to them. Needs are varied and so are the settings required to fulfil them. All too often, youth work is delivered by means of the traditional club or centre. Other building-based provision such as drop-in coffee bars, information kiosks, counselling and advisory services, community workshops and emergency accommodation is both poorly provided and inadequately resourced. Few locations offer the range of facilities required. There are exceptions: the city centre project in Milton Keynes incorporates self-contained flats, emergency accommodation, a social centre, an information service with a kiosk plus Viewdata screens in different parts of the city, a counselling service, a young arrivals service providing information to all young people who move to the area, and detached work.

Social and political education

Social education has been defined as 'the conscious attempt to help people gain for themselves, the knowledge, feelings and skills necessary to meet their own and others developmental needs' (Smith, 1982, p. 24). Developmental needs remain with us throughout our life but at times of growth and change we may be more aware of them than at others. The transition from young person to adult during adolescence is a period of great growth and change. Young people, for example, are becoming physically mature, entering into sexual relationships, leaving school, encountering the world of work or unemployment, leaving home and becoming legally entitled to do certain things. The worker's role with young people during this time is to help them meet their own needs and the needs of others in a social or societal setting. It is about being aware oneself as an individual and relating appropriately with those around one. Self-awareness, openness to change and sensitivity to others would all be aimed for.

Social education historically provides a major philosophical basis for youth work and most youth work agencies today cite the provision of it high in their list of aims. However, the traditional emphasis on self-awareness and personal development on its own was felt to be inadequate as newer and more radical forms of work broke through in the 1970s. Work with girls, ethnic minorities and other groups of young people who were clearly disadvantaged in relation to other members and groups in society, stated loud and clear that it was not merely personal awareness and change that would be required to obviate their various oppressions. Political awareness and structural change were felt to be crucial. Young women in consciousness-raising groups, black and white young people in the Rock Against Racism movement, the young unemployed on the People's March for Jobs, young homeless campaigning against social security regulations through localised HASSLL (Homeless Against Social Security Lodgings Limits) groups have all provided evidence of this increased awareness and struggle for change.

Today, the provision of political education for young people has been cautiously, if somewhat grudgingly, accepted. Whether its actual practice is widespread is another matter. Concerned as it is with making young people aware of the concept of power, of the existence of power relationships within society, whether between two people or between groups, it hopes to develop an understanding that within any setting some have more power and are stronger than others. For many workers it is also concerned with encouraging young people to participate, to take part in and influence others in making decisions, and to act collectively as a means of increasing their individual power. For others, political education can have a controlling function; showing people their position in society in relation to others and maintaining them there.

Social and political education can be viewed as two opposing ends of the youth workers' educational spectrum. The traditionally adopted social educational approach says that problems facing individuals are their own fault and it calls on them to change in order to cope or fit in better. In other words, it views young people themselves as problematic. The young person who disrupts the classroom comes to be seen to be the problem rather than institutional factors. The problem of youth unemployment comes to be seen as the fault of young people themselves rather than as the initial absence of jobs. Money is thus invested in further training rather than in the creation of more work.

The political education approach emphasises more the position of the young person in society in terms of their class, gender and race, for example. It looks at the external factors that may be affecting them as a result of their position, such as poverty, sexism and racism. It views them as active participants, themselves having the potential ability to effect change.

It will be seen from the above that links can be made with the immediate problems that affect and confront young people and with wider concerns. It is the concept that for many private troubles there are also public issues. Thus the private trouble of the young person unable to find accommodation can be linked with the public issue of there being a lack of adequate housing provision for the young single homeless. A failure to think politically and make these links signifies a conscious orientation toward inaction on the part of workers.

For some youth workers a clear distinction exists between political education and political action, whilst others take the view that political education is political action. It is the fear of political action that makes many antagonistic to the concept of political education and to state their belief that education should remain free from politics. The alleged 'political bias' of certain workers, the 'lack of balance' they provide in presentation of their attitudes and beliefs, and the subsequent 'indoctrination' of those with whom they work adds fuel to the fire. Allowing the putting up of CND and People's March for Jobs posters, allowing political statements in a young persons' magazine, and even encouraging young people to vote for any party at an election have all created problems of this kind.

However, this ignores the fact that organised education is already politically loaded, lacks balance, is biased and very definitely indoctrinates young people into acceptance of a predetermined set of attitudes and beliefs, and into acceptance of an arguably unequal, unjust and unfair society where the greatest amount of wealth, resources and power are held and wielded by a small minority. It also views young people as totally mindless beings with no ideas, values and beliefs of their own and no ability to argue their own standpoints and make up their own minds.

It is true that traditional closed styles of education have taught young people to accept passively that which is passed down to them from a higher authority and that these styles can and are adopted by certain workers in youth work settings. Adoption of an open style in which young people are encouraged to question, confront and challenge workers in the same way that they themselves are questioned, confronted and challenged may encourage rejection of what is viewed as unreasonable dogma.

We are in danger of indoctrinating young people if we allow our biases to totally exclude other viewpoints or positions from being aired. It is possible to find that being open about personal biases with others: co-workers, managers and management committees, can act as a check if we are adopting positions counter to the accepted aims and values of education. This occurs if we experience a supportive, accepting style of management. However, if the management is of a more authoritation kind, such disclosures could place us in an extremely vulnerable position.

Methods of social and political education

Within a framework of social and political education we can distinguish many ways through which workers consciously attempt to change young people or to move them on. Within these it is possible to distinguish five main methods: role model,

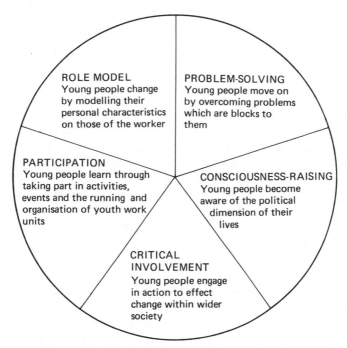

Figure 4.1   *Methods of social and political education*

participation, problem-solving, consciousness-raising and critical involvement. It must be stressed that these are not separate methods carried out one at a time by workers, for they are all interlinked and part of each other. What is suggested, though, is that if youth workers are indeed educators, all these methods should be components of their work.

Moving young people on through a role model

Quite simply, this is where young people learn ways of behaviour, thought and action through the contact they have with adult workers. We have seen earlier how attitudes, values and beliefs can be taught whether we intend it or not. This is particularly so with young people who are involved in the process of establishing an adult identity. For many workers, being, thinking and acting in a certain way is not often thought about as a conscious means of moving people on. However, our actions are frequently far more powerful than our words could ever hope to be. The adoption by a worker of a particular style of working and living can be a most effective way to demonstrate to young people that there are alternative ways of being to those propounded through traditional sex- and race-role stereotypes.

Male workers all too often assume a role of dominance and superiority within youth work settings. Whilst they are busy playing pool, darts, football video games or whatever, most frequently with the boys, the menial housework-like tasks of serving behind the coffee bar, preparing food and cleaning up are left to the women. Reinforcement of the typical male role thus occurs. Male workers who consciously take on their fair share of such tasks and female workers who will not accept such subordinate roles help project the message of a much greater equality between the sexes.

Likewise, if we shout and bawl at young people as a result of their behaviour we are, in fact. acting, albeit psychologically, with violence towards them. We project the image that when frustrated, either with ourselves or with others, it is acceptable to act in such a violent way. The cycle of aggression, with youth workers shouting at young people and they in turn taking it out on others or through acts of vandalism, is encouraged. By attempting to act, even in the most difficult circumstances, with a guiding philosophy of concern and respect towards others, there is a strong possibility of breaking that cycle. By attempting to follow this principle, however difficult, the long-term effect is positive in terms of relationships with young people.

Moving young people on through participation

Most learning that takes place within the Youth Service is experiential. By taking part in a range of experiences, some structured and some not, the young people increase their knowledge, become more aware of their feelings, and develop skills. Opportunities for participation in a youth work setting range from conversation, either with peers or with an adult worker, through activities and events within the establishment or the wider community – sports, crafts, drama and trips away, for example – to the organisation and running of the establishment or project itself.

The more formal the youth work the greater the emphasis likely to be placed on structured participation, for example, by means of programmes of activities and events, members' committees, representation on management committees, and young people taking on specific work roles or areas of responsibility. Less formal settings are more likely to lay emphasis on a more spontaneous and opportunistic approach to participation. Such opportunities may arise out of discussion, an event or a particular desire by an individual or a group to do something, rather than it being pre-ordained.

Encouraging the increased participation of young people is here regarded as an important and valuable method within youth work. It emphasises both the social – taking part and doing things with others – and the political. The organisation and running of an establishment, for example, brings into question a whole range of concepts such as control, power, resources, authority, responsibility, conflict, decision-making and many more, as well as enabling the development in individuals of a whole range of skills. In terms of developing knowledge, feelings and skills of a political nature, participation is sometimes regarded as being the only method required.

But this is not the case: a full political education also involves consciousness-raising and critical involvement.

There are also limitations to this method. Not surprisingly, youth work settings tend to reflect the wider society in which they exist. Formalised participation in the running of an establishment or project by means of a committee or council, unless specifically structured otherwise, can tend to favour the articulate young person over the inarticulate, the advantaged over the disadvantaged, the majority over the minority, the relatively powerful over the relatively powerless. Here is an example from my own experience: The coffee bar at which I worked used to hold weekly open meetings. Any young person who wished to have a say in how things operated there was encouraged to attend. At one of these meetings the young people present, predominantly male, firmly decided that I had to take down the girls work poster that was up on the walls and not put up any more. Of course this was not a line of action I would have wished to follow but having set up a 'democratic' forum I was obliged to grit my teeth and comply! Pitfalls such as this need to be borne in mind when putting this particular principle into practice.

Participation in youth work settings, therefore, is nearly always on adult terms. The limits to what young people are allowed to do are most often set by adults and they are always likely to have the final say. We frequently give young people responsibility, but seldom do we give them power. For example, we might well encourage young people to become responsible for the raising of money for a youth club, centre or project. How often, though, are they themselves allowed the freedom to make decisions as to how it is spent? We frequently invite them to be members of our management committees, but how often are they in the majority? Sometimes we invite young people to attend interviews for staff but how frequently are they allowed the final decision as to who is appointed?

Moving young people on through problem-solving

We have already looked at some of the changes young people undergo during their transition to adulthood. With them come experiences, situations and obstacles that they may not have encountered previously. Many of these the young person will cope with quite adequately whilst others become problematic.

Helping young people to find ways of solving these and other problems is an important vehicle to enable them to move forward. Showing an interest in the individual at a deeper rather than just at surface level, being supportive, acting as a counsellor and guide are all-important. Problems can often be made easier for the young person to overcome when broken down by the worker. From the girl who fears pregnancy from her first sexual experience to the young person overwhelmed by school exams and the parents' expectations of them, posing the right questions can often lead them through what has seemed an impenetrable barrier.

Provision of information is also important here. What the signs of pregnancy are, how and where to go for a test, where the nearest pregnancy counselling service is available. What the options are for someone who fails their exams: staying on at school, college courses, YTS, jobs and unemployment. By offering information to the young person their power and ability to exert more control over their own lives is increased. Encouraging young people to do things they have not done before within the youth work setting is a conscious way of enabling new experiences to be confronted. Organising a disco, arranging a trip away, running the coffee bar are all daunting prospects and present many difficulties when viewed for the first time. The careful support of the young person by the worker may make it possible for them not only to overcome the area of difficulty itself, but also to gain confidence to confront further unfamiliar experiences that may occur outside the setting.

Moving young people on through consciousness-raising

Young people should be encouraged to be aware of the political dimension of their lives; to become aware of their rights, legal, economic and sexual; to become conscious of their position in society in terms of their age, class, gender and race; to become conscious of how they are oppressed, how they oppress others and their relative positions of power and powerlessness. And their prejudices as well as those that operate against them should be confronted and challenged.

Many of the newer, more radical movements in youth work, such as work with girls, rely heavily on this methodology. Becoming conscious of something is seeing something new and different in the old, familiar picture. The new and the different add a fresh perspective to our understanding and consciousness is raised by encouraging those who share a common experience, sexism, racism or unemployment, for example, to meet and consider their situation. They are encouraged to make links between experiences within their own lives and what is happening in many other people's lives at the same time.

Victims and perpetrators of sexist and racist comments and behaviour in the immediate youth work setting should be encouraged to make links between their actions and the position of women and black people in wider society. Young people who are unemployed and have little money might be encouraged to see their position in relation to others who exist in poverty, and to become aware of factors that maintain them in that position.

Moving young people on through critical involvement

When young people do become aware of their position in society in relation to others, and of the position of others in relation to them, they may wish to change their situation or that of other people. Critical involvement occurs when young people actually take some form of action in order to change things. It differs from participation in that it tends to take place outside the youth work setting. It can be seen as 'highly acceptable', for example, voluntary community action to benefit worthy causes; 'moderately acceptable', such as writing letters to newspapers or lobbying MPs; or it can be seen as 'highly unacceptable', for example, in the case of support for 'unpopular causes': strikes, sit-ins, riots and other disruptive actions.

To the extent that society progresses by the critical involvement of its members, or fails to progress by lack of such involvement, youth workers should be keen to include it as an important educational method with the young people they work with.

Conclusion

Many factors can act as constraints upon youth workers, preventing them from fully carrying out their role as educators. Ill-defined policy, poor management and lack of adequate resources can be some of them. Expectations of young people themselves, some of whom may have been well and truly turned off the concept of education and who see workers and facilities mainly in social and leisure terms, can be a further limiting factor. Perhaps the biggest constraints are those provided by workers themselves. For years the Youth Service has been regarded as the poor relation within the Education sector and for the public at large the youth worker is often solely viewed as the person who runs the club and takes the kids away on camping trips twice a year. All too often youth workers have meekly gone along with this simplistic image. Many still do.

It is now time youth workers thought more seriously about their philosophy and practice. It is time they restated their case and pushed themselves forward to the very centre of the educational forum. If the belief is held that each component part effects the whole, it can clearly be seen that good youth workers cannot only aid young people in working towards transforming their lives, they might also make inroads towards the transformation of society itself.

5

Youth Workers as Caretakers

CAROL STONE

It's Bank Holiday Monday, and Mary who is a full-time youth and community worker, is settling down to her evening meal when the phone rings. The caller is a resident who lives near Mary's centre. Some young people she knows have just been to her house to tell her that the door of the centre has been kicked in. The woman has tried to contact the caretaker of the building, but apparently she's on holiday this week. Will Mary come over? Mary isn't sure she wants to, but if the caretaker's on holiday, there really isn't anyone else. Regretfully she abandons her evening at home and sets off.

Gina is a full-time worker based in a school. Since she took up post there she has been expected to cover evening activities such as community groups and adult education classes, although she is primarily responsible for the youth work. 'Cover' encompasses the collection of fees, support of staff and issue of equipment. Gina is perpetually unhappy about this use of her time; the matter comes to a head, however, when she's asked to tutor on the authority's initial course for part-time workers. The head of the school feels strongly that her absence will be detrimental and that she cannot be spared for a night a week. He refuses, as her day-to-day line manager, to agree to her doing the course.

At a time when there is an obvious need for an innovative, educational and politically-conscious youth service, to suggest that some workers spend a great deal of their time executing a caretaking function might seem, at the very least, frivolous, if not heretical. Yet the spectre of the blue-coated, key-rattling school janitor lining up chairs, changing light bulbs and sweeping up after activities is one which we have not quite exorcised. For many youth workers the image may be more sophisticated: administering letting procedures, being 'on duty', 'increasing access' by users are terms which may have a more familiar ring. However, ultimately, these are often functions of the same ilk; they are tasks which revolve around the upkeep, maintenance and protection of plant rather than the social and political education of people.

The purpose of this chapter is to examine some of the ways in which the caretaking role is made paramount for many youth workers because of the structures and situations within which they work. Whilst idealistically and professionally committed to political and social education, workers find themselves pressured into carrying out a variety of practical and sometimes very menial chores on a regular basis.

The term 'caretaker' is one which brings to mind the custodian of a building and will be broadened out here. Other interpretations must be mentioned: child-minders, social workers, nurses and police are all 'takers of care' and their roles are regularly confused with the less widely comprehended one of youth worker.

It is important in this process not to ignore the origins of the Youth Service. Historically, the term 'warden' featured in many job descriptions, nor is it yet defunct in the 1980s. The *JNC Report for Youth Workers and Community Centre Wardens* perpetuated the use of the word, which conjures up images of 'caretaker', and is further reminiscent of building manager, key-holder and institution-minder. Furthermore, whilst being born in a spirit of social control coupled with fear of a growing class consciousness, the early Youth Service manifested itself in institutions which were geared towards the social welfare of those who constituted the threat.

The early Youth Service sought to take care of young people: their morals, their leisure time and their welfare. It must not be forgotten that many of the institutions which perpetuated this early service are still in existence today; many of those who are involved in managing and supporting the Service in the 1980s have experience of those organisations from their own adolescence.

The legacy of the early philosophy of social welfare and

activity provision is still felt by workers, particularly within institutions which were founded early this century. Workers are still based in and employed by boys' clubs, for example, whose managers were often members and came up through that movement. A worker in such a club explained:

> The management committee have traditionally appointed a centre warden. The person before me was here for over twenty years and was very much of the old school, so he went along with their expectations. This means that they still consider my responsibilities to be the care and maintenance of the building, banking their money and running an activities programme for lads.

The polarity of opinion which exists between this worker and his management group stems from their lack of comprehension and rejection of the educational and political developments of the Youth Service. In order to maintain some semblance of a relationship with the committee, the worker must fulfil aspects of the caretaking function in order to earn their support. Attempts to build up the youth work curriculum have brought conflict if discussed. Thus, in some situations, workers are still expected to fulfil the warden/caretaker role, providing structured leisure and building maintenance in accordance with the early aims of the institution. The early history of the Youth Service still impinges upon them, being recent enough to be remembered by some of the controlling bodies.

With the Albermarle (HMSO, 1960), Milson–Fairbairn (DES, 1969) and, more recently, Thompson (HMSO, 1982) reports, the shift in the focus of the Service moved away from the social welfare model and emphasis was placed on social interaction, social education and personal development. However, this movement has been interwoven with steps to maximise links with other agencies. Youth workers are now based in schools, youth and community centres and colleges of further education. The trend towards working with youth in the community, rather than apart from it, has been a very definite and clearly identifiable one. Fewer specifically youth-work jobs are advertised, as the Youth Service in many authorities is subsumed into the Youth and Community Service, the community education service or the further education sector.

This tendency has brought into existence a plethora of neighbourhood workers, youth tutors and community education workers, whose job brief is aimed at working across the community with all age ranges, usually within the same four walls. Youth work happens as an adjunct to a variety of services whose philosophies and priorities are far from being the provision of 'programmes of personal development comprising . . . social and political education' (HMSO, 1982). Introducing informal education for young people into schools, colleges and centres which have been primarily concerned with formal teaching leads to situations fraught with difficulties. Workers in such situations are often caught up in complex management structures and are answerable to bodies of people unsympathetic to and unfamiliar with the developing Youth Service, such as school governors, college academic boards and school staff meetings which include few youth workers amongst their ranks. Similarly, conflicts may arise in community-controlled centres where provision is shared.

The lack of knowledge and empathy with youth work and its aims impinges on workers in a variety of ways. The most constant, and infinitely the most wearing, is the perennial assumption that thefts, breakages or losses within the centre are the fault of the youth club and that such acts take place as a result of evil premeditation condoned by the liberal, misguided worker. Anecdotes abound within this area: one worker was fond of combating such accusations by beginning: 'Have you heard the one about the old-age pensioners' club who ruined the new floor covering with their chewing gum?' Most workers have developed coping mechanisms against this type of allegation, be they offering frivolous or caustic comments or merely being thick-skinned. However, crises arise when the management body has the power and volition to impose sanctions to prevent use by young people, or to decree its limits.

Depressingly, both small, community-based organisations and large educational institutions seek recourse to the same measures by, for example, limiting numbers or use, excluding certain young people from membership or perhaps closing the facility for a limited period. Understanding the effects of such sanctions seems beyond many of those who impose them. Such bodies constantly contrive anger and amazement when, for instance, vandalism increases with the number of members banned. Most serious is the failure to understand that the young people who are prevented from using the facility are often those whose need is the greatest.

The following three case studies will further explore the lack of perception within the wider education service about youth work.

In Case A, an independent youth work project was established on two days a week in the youth wing of a college of further education. The college had expressed reluctance at the inception of the project but eventually allowed it to proceed for some nine months. At this point, the vice-principal decided that the wing was needed as additional classroom space, expressed concern at the disruption this might cause to the youth work, but emphasised that there was little he could do.

Cases B and C are very similar. In Case B, a college-based worker had established a daytime facility for work with young unemployed people. She was engaged in attempting to set up a young people's advice centre when the college management informed her that the youth wing was needed during the day as a student common room. It was envisaged that she, or alternatively, one of her part-time staff, would cover the session, thus decreasing the staffing ratio from approximately 1 : 10−1 to up to 1 : 50−1 : 100. In Case C likewise, the worker was informed that her daytime unemployed provision would need to close in order that the college could use the wing as a common room.

In all three of these cases, the actions taken conveyed not only a lack of awareness of the youth work process, but sought to substitute service provision and centre-minding in its place. In the cases of both B and C, the action taken would effectively exclude use by local young people in favour of recreational provision for college students, in numbers far too large for any effective youth work to take place. In both these examples the youth worker won. The facility was protected for daytime use by the unemployed, although with no guarantee that this particular battle will not be re-enacted in the future.

To dwell on the location of youth work within the formal education service throws up many examples of misconception.

The most basic are on the simple subjects of time-keeping and being on site:

> The head always expected me to turn up at 9.00 am like the rest of the staff, paying no attention to the fact that I'd often worked until 10.00 pm the previous evening. If I did come in at that time, there wasn't much I could do, other than admin., most activities didn't begin until later in the day.

> There was an incident in the youth wing and the college principal phoned me at home to ask why I hadn't been in. The fact that I'd already worked four nights that week didn't seem to carry much weight.

What prevails is a lack of understanding of the role of the youth worker and the demands which may be made upon her if she is carrying out that role effectively. To consistently expect a worker to be on site, to offer service provision and to keep similar hours to teachers is to misunderstand and misuse the resources available, and to undermine the worker's training and experience. For some workers, there is no choice as to whether to comply or not; the expectations come as directives from management.

Clashes of philosophy recur for workers within larger educational institutions. The youth worker is often the member of staff with the most flexible job description on to whom may be off-loaded a wide range of practical tasks. One worker was asked to refill the coffee machines located in the school, others were expected to do dinner duties and offer up rooms which they regularly used to school or college:

> The head asked me if he could put some children in the community room that afternoon. I told him it was used on Tuesdays for a Mother & Toddler group, and he then asked me if I could cancel it (at three hours notice) as he would like me to sit with the children.

Placing workers within such establishments without the necessary groundwork only exacerbates their being used as glorified caretakers. Heads, principals and teachers need to have some understanding of the youth worker's function before such moves are made.

Within the voluntary sector, also, misconceptions about the workers' role may create a conflict of opinions and of needs which affects the day-to-day function of many staff. A group's expectations of its employee may not always tally with the worker's ideas about the job. One neighbourhood worker's example illustrates this well:

> Several years ago, I spent some time working with a voluntary group where the mismatch between their expectations and the skills of the average youth and community worker became increasingly difficult. They were quite a dynamic local body and had acquired a building and funding for a worker. They decided to hold a meeting to establish the criteria for appointment, at which some members argued forcefully that they needed 'someone who could put in the odd window, do a bit of painting and so on'. Whilst this skill area was eventually deleted, the cleaning and letting of the building was accepted, largely because there was no one else to do it.

It would be an unjust hypothesis to state that this misunderstanding of the youth and community worker's role pertains throughout the voluntary sector. However, inadequate funding and lack of professional and practical support may have the consequence of creating job descriptions which workers find untenable.

Not totally comprehending the philosophies which pervade training and much present-day practice, perpetuates this type of conflict. The 'keeping them off the streets' view of youth work still flourishes amongst voluntary management groups, creating problems when vandalism, misuse of property or plain frustration with inadequate provision occurs. Anger and fear amongst the providers of the facility may mean that the worker who does repairs by day does little more than police the building by night. Lack of perception and lack of resources within the voluntary sector can make the caretaking role supersede all others.

Diversification of jobs within both statutory and voluntary sectors has brought for some staff an increase in administrative work. A good example of this is letting of rooms, for which many community associations and community wings have responsibility. Letting involves forms, diary keeping and billing of users, and can be a boring and time-consuming task, which will not easily attract volunteers. Thus, whilst a worker may feel that a member of a community management group could carry out this function, in practice she may find herself doing it. Letting fees need to be collected effeciently, often bringing in funding for other activities. Ideally, the task could be passed on to a clerk, but funding is not always available and in practice it is often the youth worker who carries out this task.

It appears that with more complex job descriptions youth workers are open to misconceptions about their role and function. A worker may go into a situation feeling optimistic about the broader base of the job – links with school, links with the local community – only to find that the constraints on her time are inbuilt in those areas which she originally perceived as developmental. Youth work, with its relatively short life-span, and instances of its early manifestations still in evidence, seems ever open to misconception and mistaken identity. Before examining the issue of workers' collusion with the caretaking model, there are a number of other factors which must be examined.

Whereas in its early days the Youth Service offered evening leisure provision for adolescents, it has diversified over the years and it is a common expectation nowadays that a youth centre will offer senior club, junior club and unemployed provision at the very least. A variety of activity sessions and community use may also exist alongside these. The trend towards junior and play provision especially brings with it resource implications. Junior clubs tend to attract large numbers and have different requirements from senior clubs. They are often geared to play, rather than youth work, with the implication that different skills and possibly different staff are needed. Most junior clubs operate with high numbers, low staffing and sometimes the bare minimum in terms of provision. Whilst offering facilities and activities to the members, centres are often not operating at full potential, largely due to the lack of available resources. Within many of these clubs enthusiasm and interest pervades. Nevertheless arguments that working with juniors is preparation for working with seniors carry little weight when numbers are often so high that it is impossible to hold conversations with the vast majority of those present. Child-minding rather than effective junior work is often the result.

During the last decade both professional and political pressures on workers to be seen to be offering something for the young unemployed have grown. The resource implications of this undertaking have been slow to be understood, and comprehension has coincided with cutbacks in funding which has meant many centres offering facilities on a shoestring. Workers who, for whatever reason, have not gone along the path of seeking alternative funding from bodies such as the Manpower Services Commission and the European Economic Community have tended to find themselves in the position of offering basic youth club facilities supported by the minimum staffing possible.

Within this area of work may be seen some of the most striking evidence of workers as caretakers. In many 'drop-in' centres, lunch clubs and unemployed groups we see one or two workers struggling to maintain the provision whilst at the same time answering telephones, dealing with administration and holding meetings. Being expected to fulfil one's normal daytime tasks means that the provision offered is consequently poorly supported, whilst encouraging young people to run the provision themselves often fails due to lack of necessary back-up from staff. Recruitment suffers due to lack of time, so that workers often fail to reach those young people who may need the contact most acutely.

The worker's role within this area may often be limited to opening the building, putting out equipment and being around to provide responsibility for the centre. Developmental work suffers and the worker is forced into a caretaking role. Whilst the soup-kitchen model of working with the unemployed is hardly believed to be the best, for some workers it is better than nothing, particularly if responding to needs expressed by their members and pressures exerted by management.

Underlying the issue of diversifying and extending provision to meet needs is the whole question of funding. Unless adequate staffing levels for youth workers, clerical support and caretaking hours are maintained, workers are forced into the caretaking position still further. Cuts in public expenditure have already begun to bite in some areas. When cuts come the temptation is often to maintain youth work hours with the minimum clerical and caretaking support possible. A further manoeuvre is to attempt to maintain the same level of service with less staff – a point at which caretaking and policing becomes paramount and youth work falls into abeyance.

Underspending on youth service is already an established fact. The recent report *GREA Today: Gone Tomorrow?* (Smith, 1984) shows that funding allocated for youth work is being directed into other areas of local government expenditure in seventy-eight of the ninety-six English LEAs (1982/3 figures). As the Youth Service loses out on its funding to the benefit of other sectors of the Education Service, ways to pare down provision are sought out.

Authorities engaged in the process of cutting back youth provision tend to use the head-counting model. A club which is deemed successful is one which brings in the highest number of young people, preferably with the lowest amount of attendant 'aggravation'. Ratios used by authorities for staffing vary considerably – 1 : 15, 1 : 20, 1 : 30 amongst them. Small group work, counselling and regular one-to-one contact with members is undermined by such high and inflexible ratios. Discos, sporting events and basic leisure provision often exclude the possibility for real contact with young people. The youth workers are consequently forced into the building manager/ policing model at the expense of social education, counselling or basic friendly contact.

With such pressures upon them youth workers clearly don't always have the choice as to the model of work they pursue. Necessity often dictates opening up with minimum staffing and policing facilities rather than working with kids. The question of how far workers collude with the caretaking model is thus a difficult one to answer. Acceptance of the caretaking role manifests itself in all manner of ways. It is impossible to sift all the claims to overwork, understaffing and excess administration to discover which workers have given in to pressure and which find this model easiest to operate.

The latter group includes workers whose enjoyment of the caretaking role is obvious. Having control and being 'in charge' of a centre easily supersedes all other functions, particularly when this manifests itself in giving instructions and holding keys. Keys, indeed, are a symbol of the power such workers hold; only the favoured are allowed to borrow them and in general they are handed over ostentatiously with an instruction to 'bring them straight back'. The group who are least likely to be allowed to borrow them are the young people who use the centre, whose nightly glimpse of the keys is at the point when the leader arrives and lets them into the building. Holding the keys ultimately means having control over what happens in the building, who does what and where they do it. It is a brand of power which many workers enjoy to the full, bringing deference from others and a feeling of status. This may be particularly important to those seeking managerial positions, or wishing to enforce their position as worker-in-charge. Assuming the trappings of management may be particularly important where the worker feels uncomfortable with face-to-face work, staff supervision and personal contact.

Other reasons for collusion are various. The most obvious is having a ready justification for what one does. The tangible results of youth work are not easy to perceive, let alone assess. 'Social education' is not a term which is widely used by the general public, nor is it understood entirely by some managers, heads of schools, colleges and community associations amongst them. Recognition of the nature of youth work and the process it entails is not easily forthcoming. The examples given at the beginning of this chapter exemplify the tasks that workers can be expected to carry out, however unwillingly. Combating arguments which insist that youth work is about practical tasks and building functioning can be frustrating, particularly when the proponent of those arguments has, in the end, a managerial role and can overrule the objections.

Pressure comes also from other quarters. Colleagues of different disciplines misinterpret the term 'youth worker', as do adult users who share provision:

There's really no way out of the situation that persists here. One or other of the youth work staff has to do some sort of patrol duty each night the club's open, because the adult users make complaints to the users committee every time something goes wrong. There is a constant expectation that the youth staff are here to prevent kids – any kids – from causing a disturbance. Sometimes kids who aren't members come in and cause a bit of a disturbance, but it's pointless trying to argue that this really isn't our fault. At the end of the day we're going to carry the can.

The expectation in this case that the youth workers were there to prevent disturbances means effectively that this club operated a member of staff short each night it opened; one person was always 'patrolling' the centre. Attempting to explain that this might undermine the youth work curriculum met with little sympathy: the notion that youth work staff would be better employed protecting adults than 'sitting around talking to kids' was prevalent.

Multi-purpose centres in particular generate examples of conflict between articulate adults, who feel that they are engaged in a purposeful activity, and young people, whose unstructured leisure provision they believe to be less important. The criticism comes not only from users but from adult education tutors, teachers and caretakers themselves. Reports of noise, unsupervised young people on the premises, graffiti, damage, all effected 'whilst the youth workers were just sitting around talking to a few kids' can push the worker into the supervisory, policing role very effectively. Collusion with the expectations and perceptions of the wider world may make for a much quieter life.

Then of course, there are the caretakers themselves. Often happy as low-paid workers to take the overtime associated with extended use of buildings, some of the tasks which accompany it are seen as extra to already heavy workloads. Whilst the setting out and clearing up of teaching rooms is seen to be within their brief, it is the youth and community work tasks which tend to be neglected and forgotten:

We used to run a Friday night film show for kids aged 8–13 in the school. When the word got round, we'd have upwards of 150 kids at those sessions, they were really popular. I was glad they were only once a month though, because on the Friday afternoon, I had to put out 150 chairs and set up the screen. There was no way the caretakers would do it, they used to argue it wasn't their job, so if I wanted the show to happen, I had to do it myself, or get some of the kids to come in and help.

Collusion is often born of necessity. If the work is to go on, the room must be prepared, and if no one else will do it, it becomes the youth worker's job. At the end of youth club sessions, it is noticeable that the staff sweep-up in many centres, a task which would not be acceptable to teaching staff, for example – a comment, perhaps, on the perceived status of youth work?

Collusion with caretaking is not exclusive to those based in multi-purpose centres. Workers in purpose-built and sole-use youth centres may experience and accede to very similar pressures. For many such centres operate with limited caretaking facilities. Dependence on the services and goodwill of a part-time caretaker or cleaner-in-charge may mean that sweeping-up after sessions, opening the building for groups and remaining to take care of the premises during their use are regular expectations of the youth worker:

> Our caretaker is only part-time, she comes in every morning at six to clean the building through before we come in. We have to make sure that someone's around for daytime users – we have lettings to a pensioner's group and mothers and toddlers, who we open up for so that she doesn't have to do it. If we asked her to do it, the cleaning would suffer.

This example illustrates one way of co-operating – taking on board some of the caretaking. Similarly, as work develops, pressure may be brought to bear to support the caretaker by relieving him of work:

> I've worked every Sunday for the last eight weeks. Some of the members come in to practice dancing in the mornings, and I really can't ask the caretaker to do any more hours – he does five evenings as it is, plus most Saturday mornings. So I've decided that I'll come in for a while and see how it goes.

This second example was in a centre funded by a voluntary group, so the caretaker's lack of enthusiasm for more overtime was coupled with lack of additional funding. The worker consequently became caretaker on a more expensive basis.

Workers in single-use centres are often susceptible to the caretaking role because of the limited caretaker hours available to them. Collusion is almost an imperative if the work is to proceed and develop. Whereas in multi-purpose centres caretaking hours may be available to cover other activities, single use centres' reliance on one person, who is often part-time, virtually dictates assistance with carrying out the work. Locking-up, setting alarms, sweeping-up, are all part of this process. The problems arise when the work erodes sessions and energy and other work begins to suffer:

> We really don't have enough staff to cover, let alone develop our unemployed group. Similarly, we don't form enough links with other local community groups – we don't have the time. Either myself or one of the deputies has to be here every time the club is open for something; so we haven't really time to staff any further expansion of the programme.

Dependence on a single full-time worker in this type of setting may also add pressure to be constantly on site. When 'trouble' in whatever form has been in evidence, the full-timer is expected to be around, to offer support to other staff. This expectation causes resentment by other staff when the full-timer absents herself, whether for meetings, home visits or time off. Even part-time youth workers sometimes fail to under-stand the implications of the ten-session week and full-timers are described as 'never being in' or 'hasn't been seen for weeks'. When these statements find their way to the full-timers ears, as they invariably do, the pressure is increased to be constantly on site.

This particular pressure is one which is also exerted by the young people themselves. Most centre-based youth workers will recognise and recall the hoots of derision which greet the statement 'going to a meeting' as they leave the centre just as an evening session is beginning. The full-time worker is often the person with whom most of the kids have a strong link, so seeing this person absenting himself or herself may cause resentment – it may certainly cause them to put pressure on for that person to stay.

For some workers, the caretaking function offers an escape. The pressures of continuous face-to-face sessions, of consider-ing the curriculum, of holding yet another conversation with even more young people can become too much. Administration, stock-taking, store-cupboard tidying and the like are often easier ways of passing a session than actually facing the demands of groups of young people. Escapism may be another reason for collusion.

Young people, and indeed other members of the community, tend to have a limited comprehension of the youth work role. Sitting around talking or taking young people on outings sounds and looks like a 'cushy' job to many of those who are on the receiving end. Pressured by being constantly asked, 'Is this your real job? Do you get paid for doing this?', workers may well begin to admit to being building minders and key holders, with the consequence that they start to fulfil these roles rather better than some of the others they may wish to assume. Opening the centre, setting out equipment and putting tips on pools cues may assume a magnitude which leaves little time for socially educative practice, largely because they are tasks which look more like a 'real' job which people will understand.

The expectation of young people using a youth club is that it will be available as often as possible, for as long as possible. Complaints about opening hours being too short are familiar to most workers. Having said that it's her job to look after the building, the worker finds it difficult to refuse to offer extra hours although it may perpetuate conflict between herself and the users of the provision. Development may often be desirable, but if the resources to provide it are not available, then it can only be achieved by dissipating the energies and skills of staff, which is an argument that young people seeking greater availability of provision will not readily accept.

In *GREA Today: Gone Tomorrow*, David Smith argues:

> It is an inherent part of the task of a good youth worker, paid or voluntary, to ensure that the resources to continue youth work are forthcoming. That task involves monitoring current resource levels and evaluating the effectiveness of their use in meeting the needs of young people. (1984, p. 1)

He makes the point later that the public perception of the Youth Service and what it involves is not a clear one. Both these points are pertinent to the concept of youth workers as caretakers. Until those who fund and manage youth provision are in accordance with the aims of the Service, and adequate resources are made available, youth workers will continue to be inappropriately used.

The Youth Service suffers constantly from misconceptions and ambiguity. For youth workers, attempting to fulfil the role of social educator, counsellor and developmental worker, the target group is not only the young people identified as their clients: it must also include their managers, local government officers and elected members. Only when the perception of the Service is changed in those people's minds will the Service move away from its origins and shake off the caretaking model.

6

Youth Workers and Juvenile Justice

JOHN TEASDALE and NORMAN POWELL

Many young people come into contact with the Law, as the suspects, victims or perpetrators of crime. For most this experience is both frightening and intimidating. Few are able to handle the situation well and for most it is unlikely that they will fully understand the complexity of the system into which they are drawn.

Youth workers will often find themselves becoming involved in the juvenile justice process as initiates with little fore-knowledge of what awaits them. The justice system is often seen as the preserve of the professionals, be they lawyers, the police or representatives of social work agencies. Most workers completing a typical Youth and Community Certificate or Diploma course will receive little detailed training in the judicial process. They are likely to enter the judicial arena when approached by a young person or by a professional worker to 'do something', perhaps out of some received and vague notion that youth workers by just being there are meant to help. They are then likely to become involved in 'learning on their feet' as problems arise, unaware of the potential unintended negative consequences of their interventions.

Both of us can remember our first tentative steps into the area of juvenile justice and the humiliating experience of trying to gain access to a young person in the police station without really knowing our rights and entitlements. Neither did we know how the judicial process worked or the parts that people played in it. All have been learnt by trial and error, even down to recognising the importance of the image to present in a court of law and when, and when not, to compromise.

This lack of knowledge of the judicial process is particularly unfortunate when it is remembered that youth workers have a large constituent population likely to be affected by crime. It is estimated that up to 90 per cent of crime, including juvenile crime, is unrecorded (Home Office, 1982). Research has shown that young people aged between sixteen and nineteen are most likely to be the victims of recorded crime, particularly crimes against the person (Lea and Young, 1984).

Crime is a temporary phenomenon in the lives of most young people, but it occurs at a time when youth workers may have informal links with them. Historically, juvenile offending has always existed, but detection rates and levels of crime will vary along with other circumstances such as policing policies. Despite moral panics generated by the popular Press, crime amongst the young is not a problem unique to the twentieth century or to the social conditions of the 1980s and the level of recorded crime amongst young people has decreased since 1974 in line with demographic trends (NACRO, 1985). However, society's treatment of juvenile crime has changed.

Criminologists tend to agree that the peak age for known juvenile offending is fifteen for boys and fourteen for girls (HMSO, 1983), and with minimal interference, most young people mature out of offending as they enter adulthood (Osborn and West, 1980). The exception to this applies largely to those young people who have experienced successive interventions in their lives from an early age. In England and Wales these interventions are imposed by the courts for welfare and justice reasons. They include the use of care proceedings in a variety of settings for young people from an early age up to eighteen; supervision by social workers; IT or an Attendance Centre order from age ten, the age when a young person is judged to be criminally responsible; and custody for boys aged fourteen and over and girls over fifteen. Regardless of whether these interventions are punishment, care or treatment orientated, they will rarely stop offending. At best they may reduce or control crime but they are more likely to encourage re-offending. Young people who have forced upon them the increasingly strong cocktail of care and control offered by the courts become increasingly criminalised. They are labelled, stigmatised and clientised as offenders and are more likely to head towards custody and contact with more sophisticated criminals.

The effects of labelling often start with the first appearance in court. These effects could be reduced by diverting more youngsters from court appearances, which, as Britton notes elsewhere in this book, occurs more frequently in the Scottish system. Cautioning as a successful means of diverting young people from court appearances is being increasingly used in England and Wales. A cautioning scheme developed in the 1970s in the Metropolitan Police area resulted in up to 80 per cent of juveniles who received a caution never returning to the notice of the police (HMSO, 1981) and similar success rates are recorded elsewhere.

At this point it should be noted that the justice system in general deals differently with girls and boys, often reflecting institutionalised sexism particularly in relation to sentencing practice and welfare responses. In general, boys are viewed as bad and often in need of punishment, whilst girls are viewed as vulnerable to influence or in moral danger and in need of protection. This often results in a greater percentage of girls being placed in care earlier in their offending careers and very few juvenile girls being given custodial sentences (Home Office, 1983).

Successive legislation which has effected the respective juvenile justice systems of both Scotland and England and Wales since the 1960s has represented a variety of political and philosophical viewpoints. These encompass the views of law and order conservatives, magistrates, the police and radical liberal elements drawn from the ranks of sociologists and social workers. Combinations of both welfare and justice models have been incorporated in legislation, often in an unpalatable compromise. Regardless of their intent, the overall effect of legislation and social policy in all parts of Britain has been to increase the number of offenders receiving harsher sentences. In all regions, even in Scotland with its welfare-orientated non-criminal Children's Hearing System there has been a marked increase in the numbers being placed in care or custody at a time when the relative number of adults being placed in institutions is declining. In England and Wales, for example, the number of young people receiving custodial sentences has risen from 5000 in 1957 to 32 000 in 1982, a percentage rise from 14 per cent to 37 per cent of all those receiving custodial sentences (Rutherford, 1985).

Given this deepening malaise, what positive role can the youth worker perform to retain young people who pose little risk in the community and to help them avoid court appearances, convictions and punitive sentences?

Youth workers by their very nature are a diverse breed in terms of work roles, personal philosophy and job priorities. Given other variables, notably the peculiarities of their local justice system, workers have tried several approaches. First, they have supported known individuals or groups of young people throughout their involvement in the legal process. Secondly, some workers have become involved in preventative work with young people deemed to be 'at risk'. Thirdly, workers have become involved in diversionary or delinquent management initiatives operating in their localities. Finally, and perhaps more speculatively, they have, and may increasingly, become involved in helping their constituent communities to deal with their own crime. These approaches and their advantages, plus the difficulties and drawbacks of each will be discussed in turn.

Working with consent

Some would argue that the worker should not intervene in a system in which, unlike parents, social workers, solicitors, police or teachers, she or he is the only adult who has no statutory right to do anything. But here lies both the worker's strength and weakness. The worker who becomes an advocate for a young person does so as an adult friend working with the consent of the defendant. Involvement is based on the relationship the worker has developed with an individual or his or her peers. Workers will have their own ways of gaining credibility to make the notions of encouraging participation and power less a piece of rhetoric and more a developing reality. The worker can become more of a trusted friend than an outside professional adviser. Workers will be aware of the powerlessness and confusion facing most young people in the courts and can provide a friendly safety net to encourage offenders to take decisions and calculated risks, to have a say within the judicial process and make their voices heard. The notion of consent is important as the young person is involved in a process which may be incomprehensible and which is dominated by contact with adults who are legally obligated to be involved and have their say. Against this background it is too easy for youth workers to become involved at the request of parents or social workers without the young person's consent. Wherever possible, the young person needs to be encouraged to understand their rights as well as their obligations and to understand the whole process they have entered. Youth workers are good companions to support this informally. Like any good friend acting as a facilitator, the good worker will also know how to deal with rejection and when to withdraw to discourage dependency.

Professional workers rarely spend sufficient time explaining a young person's rights and powers. Despite well-intentioned attempts at rights education, this seems to remain a rarely achieved goal for the majority of defendants. This is exacerbated because youth workers and young people only see this information as being relevant when they are directly involved in the process. Once engaged, the worker has an ideal opportunity to present the young person in a different and positive light to the professionals involved. Practical possibilities for this are discussed later in this chapter. The worker may well know the defendant far better than do the other professionals involved, but may not have the status to be listened to seriously in case reviews, or by the police, social services or magistrates. Workers will need to be assertive yet tactful enough to gain credibility to match the pomp and status of other agencies. However, as the worker gains status through increased contact with these agencies, it is important to be aware of the possible dangers of colluding with professionals against the interests of the young person.

Preventative work – preventing what?

The range of responses to juvenile crime since the 1960s has meant that youth workers have long been involved in running IT or other preventative measures. Many youth activities and organisations in various localities in England and Wales will be designated as listed facilities for statutory IT as it is offered to the court by the Criminal Justice Act, 1982. The reason for workers' involvement in these activities varies from a genuine willingness to do something for those at risk of offending or re-offending to the fact that financial resources are often more readily available for this than for mainstream youth work.

Apart from the benefits of many good voluntary (that is, non court-based) schemes for young people there are gains for workers and young people when multi-disciplinary teams come together to take on this work. Such a multi-disciplinary approach involving probation officers, social workers, police, teachers and youth workers breaking professional ranks and joining with volunteers, parents and young people themselves could potentially offer far better prospects than a decade of new legislation.

Workers need to avoid the risks of adopting social-work-type interventions earlier in the lives of young people merely because they are 'at risk' of something. There are dangers of labelling groups of individuals as being different and being perceived as such by professionals or the local community. Precisely which young people are 'at risk' needs defining. Certainly current research suggests that young people identified as requiring and receiving preventative work are no more likely to go on to offend than those who do not receive this input (Thorpe *et al.*, 1980; Lerman, 1975). There are also dangers, particularly as far as courts are concerned, if a clear distinction is not made between 'preventative work' and IT. IT is a court disposal made as part of a court order and is usually associated with statutory supervision by a social worker or probation officer. By offering a young person youth work in the guise of IT to get funding for a project, workers may well be running the risk of labelling that young person and diminishing their chances of being sentenced to statutory IT if the court considers this at a later date.

Diversion

There have been attempts since the 1970s to set up local, and in Scotland national, systems of delinquency management. One consequence of these has been to minimise young people's involvement in the judicial system. The Scottish system is based upon the Reporter's role of monitoring and gate-keeping young people's appearances in the courts and at childrens hearings. In England and Wales some local multi-agency approaches have been developed to monitor and gatekeep the system in order to divert young people from court, care and custody. The local initiative has in some areas been taken by the local authority, in others by the police or by a voluntary agency. The question of the role of youth workers being involved in these multi-agency initiatives will be considered later.

Community approaches to crime – reparation?

A very different perspective to inter-agency work from that outlined above involves the youth worker working with others in the locality to help the community deal with specific crimes through formal or informal reparation schemes.

Youth workers will usually have a clear idea of the various attitudes to juvenile crime which are assumed within the communities with which they work, be these from parents, young people, traders, the elderly and, of course, the members of management committees of youth and community projects. The current approach to criminal justice in England and Wales involves the considerable use of coercion and punishment administered through the courts on behalf of the community. This is focused on the offender and protects the victim from being involved in resolving the crime.

Centre-stage in the court process, used to deal with criminal acts, is occupied by professionals from legal and welfare agencies. The judicial process actually removes the conflict from the members of the local community directly involved. It is arguable that in some cases local communities, including the victims of crime, would benefit from dealing directly with such conflicts as a part of their lives (Christie, 1977).

A different approach which has begun to be used involves youth workers operating alongside others to facilitate local communities dealing with crime on their own terms. A criminal justice system ideally needs to contain workable forms for managing disputes, needs to produce outcomes which are seen to be reasonably fair, needs to involve negotiation and agreement between the parties involved and needs to be efficient at dealing with crime (see Wright, 1982).

It has been shown by successful reparation schemes that the current judicial system in England and Wales, particularly as it affects young people, could in certain cases make greater use of the community and develop a more participatory approach to justice involving both victims and young offenders.

Practical examples of such developments including their deficiencies can be seen in local reparation schemes which have been monitored (Blegg, 1985). Local reparation and mediation schemes are frequently developed as inter-agency initiatives and may involve the victim and perpetrator meeting each other to deal with a criminal act through a mediator who is either a volunteer or a paid worker. Here youth workers may act as facilitators, bringing victims and perpetrators together when the young person known to the worker is ready and able to deal with such a process.

Similar types of action have long been used by centre-based youth workers to deal with petty disputes, usually involving vandalism of club premises or the personal property of members. When reparation or mediation is used to deal with recorded criminal acts, it poses several dangers and challenges to youth workers. It entails the acceptance of the fact that the youth worker is to some extent an agent of social control and accepts this as a starting point to enable the community itself to take greater power and responsibility for dealing with conflicts. Other organisations, including community groups and statutory welfare agencies, would usually be involved in reparation schemes. They need to be aware of the extent to which members of the community are ready to take direct action to deal with crime. Most importantly, the workers involved must be prepared to give some of the power they have to work within the justice system back to the community and not use the notion of community involvement as a means of bolstering their own power and status as professionals. Here

youth workers, by their experience of the practice of participation developed in youth work, have much to teach the
professionals from welfare agencies.

The proper development of reparation to deal with crime in
specific cases entails the members of the community directly
involved being treated by the worker as equals. Workers need
to shed their professional drapes and be prepared to be
criticised and treated as equals for such schemes to be a success.

The issue of the professionalising or deprofessionalising of
youth work is crucial to this area. In co-operating with certain
inter-agency initiatives described earlier in this chapter youth
workers often tend to join the body of legal and welfare
professionals as they gain status and credibility in dealing with
the criminal justice process. In community-based reparation
schemes workers have the option of encouraging representatives of statutory agencies to adopt a deprofessionalising
approach, by helping local members of the community,
including young people, to deal with crime as equals with
whatever professionals are involved.

Let us turn to the juvenile justice system itself and consider
what practical interventions have been and can be made by
youth workers. It is important to bear in mind at this stage that
local practice can vary and youth workers need to take account
of this when embarking on work of this nature. The second
important point is that juveniles, as far as the law is concerned,
are all those young people between the ages of ten and up to
their seventeenth birthday. Once the young person has reached
the age of seventeen then they will be treated as an adult and
although there are many similarities between the interventions
that youth workers can make on behalf of juveniles and adults,
youth workers need to check local practice with a sympathetic
probation officer, social worker or solicitor.

To move into a new area of work is difficult even when one
has a familiarity with what it might entail, but to enter into
involvement in the juvenile justice system, traditionally the
domain of others, takes a certain courage.

When we first began to work in this area it seemed as if all of
those already involved not only wore pinstripe suits and
carried briefcases but were also highly professionalised, in-
tellectually superior and better-educated than us. We felt

alienated and powerless and could readily understand some of the emotional trauma which young people who had experienced the system described. Nevertheless, the rewards which came from a successful intervention and satisfactory outcome were uplifting and regenerating.

The drawback for us has almost always been the unpredictability of the sentence passed and it is our experience that sometimes even the best-prepared and best-defended cases can result in severe penalties, custody or disillusionment with the system. We have found some ways in which this unpredictability and alienation may be minimised, even though we can never guarantee success, not only in the courtroom but also at the time of the initial arrest.

The following sections may be useful to those hoping to deal practically with these problems. It is emphasised again that this is an approximate and bare-bones approach based on our personal experiences and local practice.

The arrest

Once a young person is arrested they will normally be taken to the local police station. Juveniles should not be questioned unless one of their parents, or an adult acting in respect of their parents, is present. Occasionally it may be a youth worker who takes on this responsibility, particularly if the offence happens outside their normal area whilst they are on a youth club trip, or if the parents refuse to attend or are unable due to other commitments. Following initially awkward and sometimes misguided attempts to be involved in this procedure in the past, youth workers should be encouraged to be aware of the procedures and the young person's rights in this situation. This information has now been published in many forms and the National Council for Civil Liberties' Factsheets in particular have proved very useful. Whilst at the police station, juveniles will normally be asked to make a voluntary statement or the police may write out in longhand a question-and-answer interview. We have discovered the need to observe the accuracy of what is written and would also recommend advising caution to any juvenile. For example, police officers during question-

and-answer interviews may write their questions in BBC English but record the replies in dialect. Consequently, when this is read out in court as part of the prosecution evidence it may give the possibly erroneous impression that the young person was disrespectful.

A voluntary statement should only be made where there is established guilt, for example, where there is no question regarding who committed the crime. Young people always have the right to remain silent if they choose to do so and co-operating with the police does not have to involve implicating oneself. One of the drawbacks of taking on the responsibility of remaining at the police station whilst the questioning takes place is the amount of time that may be involved.

Seeking legal representation

Following the initial arrest, youth workers can assist young people if they have not already done so by directing them to solicitors in their area who specialise in cases involving juveniles. All young people should be advised to seek legal advice. Many solicitors will offer a fixed-fee interview which allows thirty minutes' advice for £5 or less. In many cases Legal Aid may be granted by the magistrates. This means that the cost of engaging a solicitor to defend a young person will be dependent on the income of the accused's parents. Almost all families dependent for their main income on state benefits will be entitled to free legal advice and representation. If a young person's parents do have to pay towards the cost of Legal Aid the amount will depend on factors such as income and savings, or how many children are in the family.

It can be particularly important to find out which solicitors are competent advocates and genuinely interested in the welfare of young people, as the way in which a case is represented can have a significant influence on the outcome.

Involving the professionals

In the case of all juveniles arrested for commission of a criminal offence the police will normally notify the local social services department of the arrest via a form called CYP1. This form will give brief details of the date and time the offence was committed, a resumé of the circumstances of the offence, name of the arresting officer and the names of any co-accused involved. Social Services or Probation departments have three weeks to respond to this CYP1 form and, generally speaking, if a young person is known by an individual social worker or probation officer and they feel the young person should not be prosecuted they can respond, giving reasons for their decision. Some Social Services departments have tried to increase the potential effectiveness of this opportunity to divert young people away from criminal proceedings by visiting every referral and making an assessment of the young person and their circumstances so that they can respond with up-to-date information. In other areas the forms may be ignored almost completely with the exception of a response in the case of one or two known individuals. Many areas have now set up Juvenile Consultation Panels with the police in order to try and prevent certain juveniles coming before the courts. Youth workers who are aware of a young person having committed an offence and feel that it would not be in the interests of that young person to appear in court have, with the permission of the young person, approached the relevant social work or Probation department and stated their case for non-prosecution, often with rewarding results. It has even been possible with the co-operation of the professionals involved to attend the local Juvenile Consultation Panel and present either a verbal or written report outlining their reasons for not drawing that young person further into the juvenile justice system.

In almost all cases where a Social Enquiry Report is prepared the youth worker, again with permission of the young person, is in an ideal position to make a positive and constructive intervention. The worker can approach the social worker or probation officer who will be responsible for the preparation of the report and inform them that they are in contact with the young person concerned and that they will be able to make a positive contribution to assist in the preparation of the report.

As social workers will be aware, Social Enquiry Reports usually consist of a range of information about the young person which will generally deal with family background and home circumstances, school attendance and behaviour, how the young person spends his or her free time, whether the young person suffers ill health or any disability, and in almost all cases the report should contain a recommendation to the magistrates as to the most appropriate sentence. A range of sentences are available and these include conditional discharge, fine, Attendance Centre, Detention Centre and Youth Custody. Two more sentences are often used in the juvenile court and these are generally welfare-orientated. These are a Supervision Order with or without specific conditions, for example IT, and a Care Order. However, this does not mean to say that they are necessarily better. Youth workers should be aware of the powers of the courts and how, in their locality, these powers are used. Workers will soon realise that some juvenile courts will operate an unofficial 'tariff' system. This means that a juvenile will receive successively more severe sentences at each new court appearance, sometimes irrespective of the seriousness of the crime. Other juvenile courts may operate a system whereby particular offences will almost always receive the same sentence. For example, dwelling-house burglary in a particular area may always result in a custodial sentence being passed unless there are exceptional mitigating circumstances.

In most cases where the young person is prosecuted and pleads guilty to the offence then a social enquiry report may be prepared with the agreement of the young person's parents. In cases where a 'not guilty' plea is to be tended a social enquiry report will not normally be prepared. There are several reasons for this, but primarily if someone has committed no offence then to make assessments regarding their home circumstances, or recommendations as to how they might be appropriately sentenced would be irrational, unjust and an affront to their civil liberties.

Social enquiry reports can be subjective and can contain value judgements which youth workers may wish to question. Many reports are prepared on a basis of information gleaned from only one or two contacts with the young person concerned. Youth workers can and do prove a valuable source of information. They should look for co-operation from the author of the report but should be careful not to collude.

Should the author of the report prove uncooperative and disinterested then a solicitor acting in the case may welcome information from the youth worker. Alternatively, a worker may decide independently to present a short character reference about the young person to the Clerk of the Court. In this case, what is written should be objective, concise and based on sound knowledge rather than on hearsay.

It is important that youth workers should only make a contribution if they have something positive and constructive to say and this should always be made with the permission of the young person and his or her parents. As part of gaining a young person's consent he or she should have free access to what is written and also have the power of veto.

School-based reports

In addition to the social enquiry report most juvenile courts would expect a report from the individual's school if any of the accused are students. Those who work in educational establishments and school-based youth clubs are in an ideal position to make a worthwhile contribution in this case. School reports can be very damaging and often there is no opportunity for the young person or the parents to read what has been written about them. Many reports concentrate on the negative aspects of a young person's character rather than look for positive features. School reports have occasionally been no more than a 'tick list' consisting of labels such as 'truant', 'bad influence', 'disruptive', 'easily led' and 'anti-authority'. It is possible for those with influence in schools to redress the balance or at the very least qualify and put into context some of these comments and argue for greater access and less 'confidentiality'.

Familiarity with the magistrates and juvenile courts

Once a decision has been made to prosecute a young person the court date will be fixed and youth workers again can make a very real contribution. Many young people and their parents find court appearances intimidating and alienating. Youth workers with a knowledge of how courts work will be able to offer some support and assistance. This can be achieved by visiting local magistrates courts, sitting in the public gallery and familiarising themselves with the functions and procedures of the various roles that people fulfil. With regard to the juvenile court there is no free access to the general public but youth workers may seek permission to sit at the back of the court by contacting the Clerk to the Court in writing. Alternatively, they may ask a sympathetic social worker or probation officer if they can accompany them. Many parents and young people do not fully understand the workings of the court system and often the language used in the court will easily be misunderstood by them. Youth workers who are familiar with the system can assist by explaining the court routine. It is also helpful if young people know that there is someone in court who is sympathetic and supportive and workers can make a positive contribution by accompanying young people.

Intervention following sentence

Once a young person has been sentenced by the juvenile court youth workers can continue to give assistance and support on a practical level, particularly if a young person is given a custodial sentence. Most people in custody attach great importance to receiving letters, and youth workers who have developed a relationship with a young person can help by writing to them on a regular basis and keeping them up to date with local news and events, or they can encourage others in the youth club to write and keep in touch. In addition youth workers can seek permission to visit a young person outside the normal visiting hours. This can be done through a social worker or probation officer involved in the case, or the youth worker, acting independently, could write to the governor of the detention centre or youth custody centre requesting permission for a special visit. Finally on release, youth workers can give much support and assistance by helping young people to take their place once more in youth club activities and friendship groups. Young people who are subject to fines can be assisted in a practical way by youth workers being aware of the financial obligations they are under and not exerting undue pressures on them to be constantly paying out for items such as youth club trips, entrance fees and youth club membership monies.

Conclusion

It is important that intervention should only take place where it is felt to be really necessary; workers should know the purpose of their intervention and ensure it does not have negative repercussions. Minimal intervention is often the best policy. Many young people are the victims of crime as well as the perpetrators and youth workers should not set apart the young people who appear before the courts and those who do not. All intervention should be freely offered and only pursued with the full consent of the young person.

The other baseline for intervention must be to ensure that young people do not become the subjects of custodial sentences in all but the most serious cases. Rutherford (1985) has identified ten features of custody for young offenders:

1. Disruption of or severance from family, employment and relationships.
2. Removal from normal maturational experience (including retardation of psychosexual development).
3. Reinforcement of criminal attitudes.
4. Enhancement of criminal skills.
5. Introduction to accomplices in crimes.
6. Experience of violence and intimidation.
7. Lessons in racism and intolerance.
8. Risk of inducing dependency on institutional life.
9. Envelopment in the suspicion afforded to ex-inmates of the prison system.
10. Stigma and social and personal consequences of a custodial record.

It can be argued that several of these features are apparent in lesser disposals available to the courts and are usually experienced earlier in a delinquent's career. For example, activities in attendance centres to which young people can be sentenced under police supervision from the age of fourteen for two-hour periods on Saturday afternoons to a maximum of twenty-four hours, bears many of the hallmarks of the short, sharp, shock administered in detention centres. Even residential care, which is frequently recommended by social workers early in the life of 'offenders', often for the best possible care and control motives, can exacerbate problems. Given the worst of residential experiences, the young person in residential care may well become associated with the first eight of Rutherford's ten features of custody.

In dealing with the impact of crime, youth workers need to be aware of the extent to which some of Rutherford's features of custody are an everyday part of growing up in the communities in which they work. Young people, particularly those who are heading towards custody because of the frequency of their offending, should be diverted to positive non-custodial options wherever possible. It is here that the youth worker and others can help in ensuring that community resources are available to help young people, their families and their communities to deal with crime.

7

Youth Workers as Casualties

FRANK BOOTON

The casualty syndrome is not an uncommon feature of youth and community work. Because of the comparatively small size of the occupational group, the actual number of professionals who become casualties is small. Youth and community work apparently has always created its casualties. There are particular identifiable features of this work that positively encourage a complex of personal and professional problems which lead to distress and/or breakdown in some individuals. It is suggested here that these are permanent features of the work. Moreover, although certain individuals may be especially prone to these effects, the possibility should be rejected that an individual pathology can wholly account for such problems.

It is important that the phenomenon of the casualty is defined with some precision. The term as used here applies to anyone who has been employed in youth work full-time and who has experienced difficulties directly attributable to the work which have led to illness, personal distress or the termination of their employment. Case studies of individuals cannot be reported in detail, but briefly they include workers from several local authorities, both male and female and within an age-span of early twenties to mid-forties. For example, Mr A is forty-four, youth-work trained, with almost twenty years face-to-face experience; his career came to an abrupt end when he had to choose between it and his marriage. Mr B is thirty-two, teacher-trained, with ten years experience; he was dismissed following misconduct involving teenage girls. Case C is a young (twenty-four) male graduate worker of 'great promise': his personal life 'disintegrated' as a result of his over-involvement in his work; he left youth work for the more professionally stable environment of teaching. Case D is a 25-year-old female American social work graduate working on a girl's project in New York. Her case is relevant because it demonstrates the current expectancy of 'professional burn out' in the American welfare scene, and anticipates certain conditions of employment that are increasingly occurring in Britain. At the time of her interview D was receiving medical attention and was about to have her contract of employment rescinded. Case E is a male worker in his late twenties who was 'invited to resign' from his statutory post after a series of problems culminating in financial mismanagement. A year after resignation he remained unemployed, receiving medical help and awaiting a recommendation for psychotherapy. Other cases on record include female workers who became clinically depressed, and others who were, like Case A, ultimately faced with 'the job or the marriage choice'.

There seems to be no typical individual that is prone to the casualty syndrome, though there are some distinctions of condition and cause between male and female. These will become apparent. Case A is an example of the anti-social nature of working conditions. A and his wife both believe that the large number of evenings spent away from home over twenty years has prevented him from being an 'ordinary' father and husband:

> We sometimes had to work round the clock. When I started here fifteen years ago we often worked five evenings a week, even seven . . .

Another range of problems concerns the 'general pressure' of a highly diversified professional task, often with complex demands, conflicting expectancies, meagre resources and limited support. Case B said:

> The whole job was pressure, every aspect of that centre had to be sorted out. The kids, the programme, the part-time staff, the coffee bar, the management committee, the building – even the caretaker – *everything* had to be turned inside out and started afresh . . .

Case C demonstrates a further range of difficulties: the lack of appropriate training. He described it as 'survival skills', though the deficiency is more complicated than that. As a trained teacher he could function well as a full-time assistant, but when his centre was reduced to single-worker status he simply could not cope with its existing pattern of operation:

> When the Senior Worker left I was working about 12 sessions a week, we both were. Within a fortnight of being on my own I was doing 18 to 20 sessions a week: yes, I was in the centre every single day and evening. The centre was very busy; we were running a 20 out of 21 sessions a week programme, that is, 3 sessions a day for six and two-thirds days a week.

The training implications here are not simply related to the skills of the worker. He was shrewd enough to recognise his emerging problem and sought help from his Area Youth Officer who was himself sensitive in his investigation of C's individual difficulty. The nature of this intervention of the part of the officer is important. It was not a counselling function that was being affected, but rather one of evaluation and support. Unfortunately it seems to have depended completely on the acumen of the officer, in this case a very experienced professional. At the point where he was contacted the officer had the sense, the skill and the sympathy to read the warning signs. Another set of problems is identified in the case of D. The typically American conditions of her job are becoming increasingly common in this country. She confessed that when she took up her post she had no real idea of what it might entail; her employers had simply 'seized a lump of money from the Poverty Programme and advertised a job'. The girl members of the project were all high risk youngsters living more or less permanently on the streets. D's job involved negotiating between young people, the police, parents, courts and social workers, but at the same time she was expected to run the drop-in centre. D became enmeshed in a situation whereby her job came to dominate her whole life. With the exception of one long weekend visiting her parents, D admitted to not having a single day free from work for over six months.

She was convinced that the agency had employed her knowing that 'after three years I would be burned out anyway'. She goes on:

> The [agency] aren't to blame . . . they have enough money to employ a worker and nothing else . . . after that . . . they will open up another, similar project somewhere else.

There is one more category of problems that should be indicated, and these can be seen in the case of E. The financial mismanagement happened because he temporarily lost control of his own behaviour due to the general pressures of his job. He experienced quite intense stress in this, his first appointment. He was conscientious to the point of personal anxiety and when the problems of the centre ran beyond the level of his skills and local support system his anxiety became so extreme that he lost the normal ability to regulate his own conduct at the ethical boundary between right and wrong. There was certainly money missing, the auditors estimate was £350, but E did not steal it, he simply 'got the money mixed up'. As he put it:

> I have not stolen anything in my life before. I don't think I have even broken the law before. I don't know what happened . . . [or] . . . where the money went. I certainly don't seem to have spent any of it.

For E, personal and professional priorities lost their distinction and he slid into a pattern of behaviour which, prior to this incident, anyone who knew him would have considered most unlikely.

To summarise at this point: there are, then, five types of 'symptom' which appear in the making of a casualty. These are largely job-derived, are interrelated, and may be found together in individual cases. They are:

1. the antisocial hours and conditions usual to the work.
2. the 'general pressure' problem; the complexity and diversity of the task.
3. the lack of certain training and absence of support.
4. the short-term expediency rationale of urban-funded project work.

5. the particularly difficult conditions of some posts which require additional training.

The making of a casualty

After this brief review of some case histories it can be seen that the casualties suffered to the extent that the normal pattern of their lives was altered. This change might be temporary, or in severe cases a permanent alteration from which the recovery of a 'normal' life might not be possible. The actual suffering may take the form of an illness, either medical or psychological, or both, or be reflected as a series of personal difficulties such as marital problems or occasionally uncharacteristic, even criminal, behaviour. We should examine some of these briefly before exploring the sense in which all of them have a direct relation to the individual's work. The person suffering medical symptoms is the easiest potential casualty to identify. The most common range of work-related illnesses are those ailments which result from the persistent disruption of social or domestic routine. B spent a lot of time at his centre, to the point where he was 'missing meals and making do with a cup of coffee and a Mars bar'. His smoking increased from fifteen cigarettes to 'about fifty' a day. Similarly, C was very busy. He could remember going home at night after eleven o'clock 'physically exhausted and mentally shattered', yet he could not sleep. D suffered the same effects as B and C, and eventually had to take medication for insomnia. She had an unhealthy, rapid weight gain, largely the result of living mainly on junk food. E also had insomnia problems and was prescribed sleeping pills. He lost weight quickly, the result of hardly eating at all. The most frequent medical conditions arising from job difficulties are comparatively trivial, so much so that the individual worker often does not attribute them to the job at all. Poor diet, hasty meals, inadequately prepared meals, 'junk food', all these are quite common. In addition there is the problem of irregular eating such as lunches taken at three or four in the afternoon and heavy suppers at eleven in the evening. The 'cup of coffee and Mars bar' habit that Case B speaks of is not at all unusual. For the younger worker this may not amount to much physical difficulty, but over a period of years the effects of permanently irregular eating habits can produce a range of diet-related complaints from chronic poor complexion to ulcers. In the small sample of professional workers from which this research is taken many complained of sleep-related illnesses also. The problem that Case C spoke about, of going home late at night physically exhausted and 'mentally shattered', yet having to sit up until two or three o'clock simply to unwind, is not unusual. Many youth workers will know of this pattern of late sleeping. The individual tends to go to bed late and consequently gets up late the following morning. This becomes the pattern for those four or five evenings per week when they are working and is very often carried over into the two or three evenings per week when they are not. Most individuals have their own strategies for dealing with this problem, ranging from unwinding to music or a video film to temporary courses of sleeping pills. In one case a GP had prescribed muscle relaxants which the youth worker used intermittently whenever she went through a period of bad sleeping. Instances of long-term tranquillization were rare, though a long-term but irregular dependency on some form of sleeping aid is not: 'I just take a Dalmane now and then, whenever I have a bad night, but I haven't taken them regularly for ages . . . '. One American worker encountered in New York practises daily meditation as a means of encouraging a relaxed attitude and behaviour, and in his case this seems to have been extremely successful as a professional coping strategy. It is difficult to predict what effects the accumulation of poor sleeping and eating habits might have on the average person, but they certainly include a general syndrome of lassitude, 'being run down', vulnerability to colds, influenza, and the usual viral infections. Whilst none of these are especially serious in themselves, the aggregate effects felt over a period of time obviously contribute to an overall lower standard of personal health. The job is likely to enhance any or all instances of poor health habit and to decrease any or all examples of good health custom and behaviour. For example, smoking may be taken in moderation, but when individuals experience difficulties those who smoke are likely to increase their intake. One worker admitted drinking 'around thirty mugs of coffee' a day. Such habits may not necessarily be addictive but they are unquestionably debilitating. Regular exercise is a typical feature of the reversion of good health habits that happen when an individual becomes unusually busy: 'I used to try and get in a game of squash every week, but things get busy, and you tend to let it go'.

The disorders which may be called 'psychological' are much harder to define than the medical category. Generally, at least in so far as this enquiry was able to indicate, the large majority of these are directly stress-derived, a factor which will be discussed later in the chapter. Common symptoms fall within a range of conditions that might generally be termed 'neurasthenic'. These include none-acute depression as the most frequent. Often the individual will quickly become so accustomed to this feeling that it will not be regarded as anything particularly unusual, and it will be attributed to a commonsense explanation that pathologises the worker:

> I just feel as though everything is too much trouble; I can't motivate myself, I seem to feel more or less permanently fed up.

The worker here was suffering from a minor bout of depression. This had been going on for several months and resulted initially from the accumulated effects of overwork during a period of time following the loss of the assistant worker post at her centre. She had simply got into the habit of working harder and longer. Eventually, a combination of physical and psychological symptoms became apparent which indicated minor clinical depression – minor in this sense meaning that the condition is not dysfunctional or debilitating to the point of breakdown. She began sleeping badly; feeling tired at night but unable to go to sleep. Her sleep was frequently interrupted and she began waking unusually early and yet still tired. She was thus starting her working day in a state of physical fatigue and over time this affected her attitude and behaviour to the point where she came to feel 'more or less permanently fed up'. She lost her appetite and consequently lapsed into irregular eating habits. She was told how irritable she was becoming, how she seemed to have lost the 'bounce' that colleagues had previously noted. Her free weekends should have been spent relaxing or recharging herself, but inevitably those completely free from work commitments became rarer. She got to the point where on those weekends when she *was* free she spent her time 'sitting around and brooding'. The fact is that such a condition is not uncommon and many people that actually suffer from such minor depression remain entirely unaware that this is the case. Another worker, again a female but in this instance one who was married with children, summed up this state succinctly:

> The other day I saw an advert that said, 'Take Aspro For That Nowhere To Park Headache': I thought, 'My God, I feel like that all the time'.

The tendency of individuals is to blame themselves, or to assume that such a condition is not at all unusual – that it is, in fact, the norm. All kinds of reasons are advanced to explain what is happening and very often the person will assume that they can 'just work through it' or 'hang on and things will get better'. This particular woman was led to believe by a friend that what she was experiencing was the onset of 'the change' (she was thirty-six) and a well-meaning colleague actually talked to her about the possibility of hormone therapy. Interestingly, it simply never occurred to her that she should go and see her doctor, so certain was she that it could be put right by 'just working through it'. An additional category of the psychologically-derived condition is that which leads to a form of breakdown, mental breakdown in fact, though many psychiatrists would almost certainly disagree with this view. This range of illnesses is difficult to describe, but includes completely uncharacteristic behaviour. The case of B is an extreme example, though the case of E is not so unusual. Both workers responded in a very personal, even self-destructive way, to a high degree of stress which was largely job-derived.

Among psychologists at present there is some debate about what stress actually is, what causes it, what its effects are and the general aetiology of the condition. Most would agree that it is a physical and psychological reaction to a set of personally-felt conditions. It can be triggered by a '. . . major disruption in a person's life; considerable interpersonal conflict; time pressures, and/or the failure to achieve major goals, etc.' (Shamoon, 1985, p. 27). However, in this sense we receive a rather narrow definition and one, moreover, that again emphasises an individual pathology. The view that psychologists take of business-derived stress, 'corporate life', as one specialist describes the context, is that middle managers are particularly prone, basically because they have in their role all the pressures of target or goal achievement without the full control over their function within the organisation. To some extent middle managers can negotiate the demands made upon them, but they cannot control them. Nor can they wholly control their own performance, since deadlines and targets are part of a commercial or industrial scene of constantly changing priorities in which the concerns of the organisation or company are paramount. The emphasis is, therefore, placed on the individual to *perform*, and modern management practice leaves the pressure of that performance largely at the individual's ability in a kind of code: a series of informal, unwritten but exacting rules, all of which ultimately apply the law of the survival of the fittest.

Some psychologists see stress in these contexts as a double-edged factor. On the one hand, the day-to-day stress of business is a stimulus to individuals to perform. It is an incentive to enhanced activity. It is also a measure of the excitement of the business environment – it 'gets the adrenalin running'. But on the other hand it becomes a psychological pollutant when absorbed in large doses, or when the individual's performance overruns his or her ability to cope with added strain. Then the individual is overextended in role, decisions are badly or wrongly made, delegation becomes indeterminate and the personal 'coping system' breaks down.

This is a commonplace view of stress. However, it is inadequate. It emphasises the individual pathology almost to the exclusion of all other considerations. Executives who can handle stress are regarded as the fittest of the tribe, those who go to pieces are seen as somehow weak, lacking in the attributes that the modern dynamic organisation requires. It pays little or no attention to the whole context of human relations within which an individual may become a victim. In certain work situations the relationships are systematically geared to producing the strong/weak syndrome because power is unfairly or unequally distributed, competition rather than co-operation is the norm, targets are unrealistic or badly plotted and support systems do not exist or are inadequate. Ultimately, the most significant stress-producing factor may prove to be the hierarchical, authority-based power structure of modern organisations. These are the conditions of the modern market-orientated industrial, commercial or business enterprise. In such contexts stress becomes a normal hazard of the role and the individual is expected to cope with it or get out:

> They are a bunch of real people around here. Tell them what you think and they will respect you for it. They don't want a man to fret and stew about his work. It won't happen to me. A man who gets ulcers probably shouldn't be in business anyway. (Whyte, 1960, p. 123)

Within such a value-framework the inability to cope with stress is tantamount to an admission of an unorthodoxy and such nonconformism is actually dangerous to the organisation.

Psychologists use the individual pathology model to construct a series of personality types, individual profiles, in order to determine which people are likely to succumb to stress. This particular line of analysis has now got a medical 'state of the art' determinism about it. 'Type As' are competitive, hostile and something which is called 'time urgent'. They are often, as Shamoon's (1985) psychologist puts it, 'jaw clenchers or teeth grinders'; they have twice the rate of cardiac disease over 'Type Bs'. They are 'corporate achievers', given to an attacking stance and they tend to perfectionism. 'Type As' are particularly prone to stress. 'Type Bs' on the other hand, are more relaxed, less achieving, given to doubt, frequently conscience-prone, less dynamic and, of course, not as good in executive positions. There is now sufficient concern about the effects of stress in the business world that a new generation of specialising psychologists has emerged and with them a range of consultancy services in what is called stress management. One privately consulting psychologist has run workshops for large corporations such as Shell, Rank Xerox, the Trustee Savings Bank and British Rail. This form of training seems to be compensatory, that is, it accepts the situation as it exists in the business environment and analyses the problem primarily from the pathology model of individual behaviour. It constructs 'coping systems' for the middle-executive which are based on the individual's enhanced understanding of his or her tendency towards the condition and the subsequent management of performance in order to avoid it. A 'coping system' will include awareness training about such aspects of the job as delegation, decisional autonomy and the individual's general homeostasis (normal equilibrium). In addition, fitness programmes, concentration on diet and an emphasis on leisure educate the executive in 'stress hygiene'. Medical screening is also now available for those whose companies wish to safeguard their staff. One particular consultant is currently the clinical director of nine separate medical centres, all BUPA registered and where, for an appropriate fee, executives can be screened both physically and psychologically. A report of this activity in the business press quoted the consultant as saying:

> We probe not only the subject's physical fitness, but also his or her basic personality and environment. This way we build up the 'big picture' – the psychiatric state of the person. (Shamoon, 1985, p. 27)

Increasing stress is certainly a feature of the modern world and unfortunately it is no longer confined to the business environment but is also becoming a factor behind individual breakdown in almost all walks of life. In the USA psychiatry and psychology have produced voluminous material on the subject and there is now a specialist study of stress available for virtually every numerically significant occupational group. In Britain, the phenomenon has only recently received widespread recognition and there is not yet a particularly large body of literature on the subject. However, each year sees much more material being produced. Trade unions in this country are becoming concerned; APEX, the white-collar union, produced a series of articles in its monthly journal in 1984 and they provoked correspondence to the point where the union felt it necessary to prepare a set of guidelines on the subject.

One very detailed study is that conducted by the Inland Revenue Staff Federation. Researchers despatched 400 questionnaires to higher grade tax officers on behalf of the organisation and received a surprisingly high 79.5 per cent return, itself an indication of the perceived relevance of the research (Labour Research, 1985, p. 147). According to the report, up to 24 per cent of females and 13 per cent of males exceeded the level of depression normally recorded for those undergoing hospital outpatient treatment. The reasons given for this high stress level were wholly job-derived, with the two most frequent causes described as 'an autocratic management style' and 'a lack of job satisfaction'.

There are no figures yet available for youth and community work but it may not be long before the professional associations or unions are faced with the necessity of quantifying the problem within the field. The Community and Youth Workers Union have been receiving an increasing number of requests from members experiencing the need for advice and guidance, and stress-related problems in the files of the Union's Casework Committee are reported to be at a high level. The sense in which a teacher, a social worker or a youth and community worker is individually prone to the condition is very difficult to predict; it is, however, necessary to acknowledge the condition as a fact of life within these occupational groups. Perhaps in so doing we can move towards a specific understanding of its condition which takes the context of human relationships more into account and does not rely for its definition on the assumption of individual inadequacies.

Professional difficulties that lead to stress

Certain types of professional difficulty are self-evident from the cases cited here. The nature of professional youth and community work can preclude the establishment of a 'normal' domestic and/or social life and in certain instances this will produce conditions for the individual within which 'ordinary' personal relationship simply cannot prevail. The job very often demands a more or less permanent system of split days whereby office or administrative work is done during the morning hours and contact or face-to-face work is done during the evenings. The typical single-worker centre-based post, assuming JNC conditions, is often thought to entail six morning and/or afternoon sessions and four evening sessions in any single week. In theory this represents what is, by the standards of industry and commerce, a short working week of approximately thirty-five hours. The nature of much of this work, especially in some urban areas, is, of course, extremely difficult. But if the work itself is productive of stress through its intensity, other problems arise from the manner in which it often has to be organised. Each working day may be split. Such a division of the day makes it very difficult to construct a firm routine to domestic or social life; moreover, the days which are worked will in the ordinary course of events tend to change from week to week. Nor does this hypothetical example assume any weekend commitments. In some centre-based posts freedom from weekend work may be possible, but for most such posts some form of weekend commitment is a regular necessity. One session each on Saturdays and Sundays (by no means an unusual occurrence) for two or more weekends per month, and the typical working week of that worker has increased from 35 to 42 hours.

It must be emphasised that these conditions are not at all unusual. In a survey of seventy full-time professional youth and community workers, the question was asked, 'In your opinion, does full-time youth work as an occupation present any particular difficulties to what you would consider a normal married life?' A surprisingly high figure of 86 per cent replied, 'Yes', with all the remainder recording 'Don't know' rather than 'No'. Interestingly, in a questionnaire administered by personal interview, it was this question more than any other that stimulated unsolicited verbal response. Almost every worker volunteered some personal information or offered comment upon the subject. The sample was random, though the majority of the respondents worked in statutory centres. Many workers were fascinated by the fact that the question was asked at all; some stated emphatically that it was 'about time that something was done', and a few (all women) confessed to having no idea that many other workers suffered similarly, the most common response being, 'I thought it was just me!' Workers with more than ten years of marriage and two or more children proved the most professionally stable in respect of 'anticipated stress', though in the worker's own perceptions, more 'at risk' in terms of personal damage if or when stress renders them a casualty. In addition, this was also the category that considered a premature exit from youth and community work the most likely solution to the problem if or when they personally encountered it.

In professional practice most youth and community workers are isolated in the sense that (a) a majority are employed in single-worker posts; (b) the Youth Service itself is a marginal operation within the public services and its relatively low status discourages inter-professional networks; and (c) the work force is usually physically isolated in that premises are few and scattered, leaving full-time colleagues with little contact at their own level of operation. This professional isolation is a traditional characteristic of the job and is one of the reasons why 'support' is a much valued feature of any youth work post. Support is widely recognised as a primary professional need of every practitioner. It is perpetually talked about in youth work, from training through to practice. Very few definitions of it have been attempted and though every practitioner comes to have an understanding of it in relation to his or her practice, when asked to define it most would respond with difficulty and/or in a wholly subjective manner. Taking these two issues of isolation and support together, this brief enquiry discovered some uncomfortable facts. Asked whether they 'had any occasion to seek confidential counsel, guidance or advice on *professional* matters arising from their work', a clear majority of workers indicated 'Yes', with multiple requests. The person chosen to consult was most often either a colleague at an equivalent level or a 'friend not involved in youth work'. No one opted for their 'supervisor'. Less than 10 per cent of respondents had access to a formal scheme of non-managerial supervision. A small number did not even know if their authority operated one. Some recently qualified workers in their first appointment were not aware if they were on probation or not. Asked to indicate the last occasion when they had professional contact with another full-time worker, excluding other workers in their own establishment (if any), the average score was more than two working days ago. Several workers scored 'more than five working days ago'. Clearly, from these limited exercises the sense in which practitioners experience isolation begins to be revealed and also the manner in which professional support is inadequately realised. At the same time it remains a real need in practice.

In such a brief examination of the issue it is difficult to do justice to the significance of the casualty in youth and community work. The aim here has been to raise the question, rather than to attempt definitive conclusions. It must be remembered that this survey was little more than a feasibility study for a future enquiry and that its limited results have been interpreted by someone without formal knowledge of medical or mental health. None the less, some implications are clear. The incidence of occupational stress is rising in virtually all categories of professional activity, and apparently no less so in full-time youth and community work. The particular circumstances of the task of the youth and community worker are such that increased levels of personal anxiety and consequent professional dysfunction are inevitable. To understand this more fully we should reject the notion that certain individuals are predisposed to suffer through their own inadequacies, and instead consider more analytically the conditions of work and the contexts of relationships within which the work is pursued.

8

Youth Workers as Entrepreneurs

GINA INGRAM

Youth workers are seldom thought of, or indeed would wish to be thought of, as entrepreneurs. The word conjures up associations which many youth workers reject. For example:

● the cult of individualism as opposed to collective or team working
● the pursuit of personal aggrandisement rather than working for and with young people
● the taking of risks for personal gain and placing others at risk against their will
● paying more attention to the large and spectacular, at the expense of the small-scale and the individual.

Entrepreneurs are usually thought of as working outside the established systems; they find a need, or a gap in the market, and move to exploit it. All of this is the very antithesis of the values attributed to youth work – these are seen by the world as being more rooted in philanthropy than entrepreneurialism. However, many of the moves forward in youth work practice have been brought about by entrepreneurs, and the negative associations of the word act to block thinking.

A definition of an entrepreneur is 'one who organises or manages an undertaking, assuming the risk for the sake of profit'. This definition has two elements: profit and risk. If the word 'profit' is not defined in the limited financial sense but widened to include other forms of gain such as status, recognition, access to personal or political power, achieving a political end and achieving facilities, access or greater educational potential for young people, then it is possible to see youth workers constructively as entrepreneurs.

The concept of risk is far harder to define. Is it risk to the young people, the worker or the organisation which is at stake? Risks exist in both physical and emotional areas. It is relatively easy to define physical risk: outdoor education, institutions and health and safety departments in the Education sector have clearly stated and remarkably uniform views on acceptable and unacceptable risk levels and yet even these areas pose problems for youth workers. Often the levels of safety required just cannot be achieved in a service which inhabits old and converted buildings and which attempts to respond flexibly, with inadequate resources, to young people's needs. As a measure of this, how many minibuses are driven each Sunday by youth workers fighting to stay awake after a weekend away with young people?

Youth work has not begun the process of defining emotional risk. Indications of this come from the total absence of discussion papers on the subject, lack of mention of the subject in youth work training and the absence of any section on risks in the literature on group exercises and simulations. As yet few youth work employers recognise burn out as an occupational hazard of youth workers.

In this uncharted area one thing is certain, an individual knows when they feel at risk, and can define for themselves the level of that risk. Thus risk becomes a matter of personal perception rather than an absolute. Things which are of high risk to one person are of little consequence to another, be they the risk of looking foolish, losing status, losing money or losing a job. As with all perceptions, individuals view risk through spectacles tinted by culture and experience. For youth workers, the relationship between funding and work being undertaken can be a critical area and can be, therefore, the focus of a feeling of risk. This assumes that effective youth work requires funding in some form or another and young people are unlikely, in the forseeable future, to be able to provide the funding for this work. Their access to money is controlled by parents until they reach an age when they either enter higher education, join a government scheme, go on to social security or begin work. The opportunity for access to money to make young people independent financially is being steadily eroded. Seen against a background of increasing youth unemployment this has implications for youth workers. Quite simply, it is impossible to work without resources and the young people themselves are less and less likely to be able to supply even a part of these resources. It follows that unless funding can be raised from new or old sources, the amount of work will decrease, or be withdrawn from those who cannot pay.

The more youth workers are involved in raising funds, the more their work can become prescribed by funders threatening to withdraw monies, and the less time they have to do youth work. The traditional argument 'but the young people can learn through fund raising activities' is true: they learn to jump through hoops to raise money! Thus the problem of the youth worker becomes one of how to raise funds and increase facilities without having the work prescribed by the funding sources in a way which is detrimental to the young people. Risk can then be measured as the degree to which youth workers' actions and practice are at variance with the values of funders. The funding sources may vary, for example, within Scouting. Sources could be considered as the public who donate funds, the local education authorities which grant-aid the organisation, the membership or the Scouting Association itself. Similarly, within the LEA sector the funding bodies can be seen strategically as the councillors, the senior officers managing the Youth Service or the communities in which the work is carried out. On occasion the interactions of these various funding bodies may be important and this point will be developed later in the chapter.

In this chapter youth work is defined as providing learning opportunities which assist and enable young people to take control of their own lives and to take an active part in the direction taken by the community in which they live. This definition to a large extent excludes leisure services and the reactive social work end of youth work, but embraces pro-active working, and real participation and decision-making by young people. It follows that it is possible to construct a theoretical grid on which any youth worker's practice may be placed (see Figure 8.1).

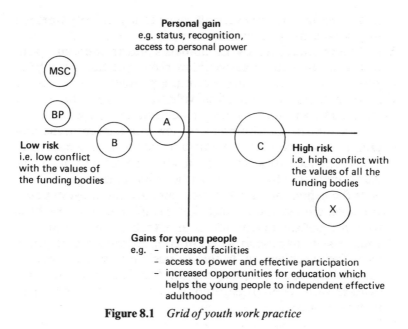

Figure 8.1 *Grid of youth work practice*

Set on the grid are six reference points. [These are placed as a result of the author's personal perspective and prejudices – others might view the positions differently.]

MSC is at one end of the scale. It represents workers who are using MSC funding to pursue youth work. This is a low risk area of work, with large opportunities for personal gain and little or no opportunity to benefit young people in the long term.

BP represents leaders of youth movements, which are in little or no conflict with their funding sources, for example, Lord and Lady Baden-Powell who initiated the Boy Scouts and Girl Guides respectively. They acquired status, access and recognition at a personal level, as well as facilities and learning opportunities for young people, by their actions.

A represents workers who operate at the reactive social work end of youth work. They work in accordance with their funding body's values, but often lack 'respectability'. Examples of this group are people who in 1920–39 ran hostels for single young women with babies, or today, people working with young drug addicts.

B is the area occupied by the thinkers and trainers of youth workers. They take relatively few risks, but can make both personal gains and gains for young people.

C is the domain of directors of voluntary organisations who push back the boundaries of acceptable youth work by supporting the development of new curriculum areas and practice in such fields as political education, sex education, anti-prejudice working and effective participation. Their work tends to be pro-active rather than reactive.

X is at the other end of the scale. Here are the most exposed entrepreneurs in youth work. This group of people are those who are considered junior within their organisation and choose to manage their work, or conduct their practice, in a way that conflicts with the values and practice of the organisation by which they are funded. They run high risks of their work being frustrated, of suffering burn out, or of being dismissed.

Obviously, it is possible to 'bend' funding towards the workers' and the young people's own agenda and away from the funding agencies' value system, but this can only be done for a limited time. The four years up to 1986 have been strewn with casualties: people who thought that they could use Manpower Services Commission funding to engage in political education, sex education and gender education.

It is interesting to record one incident in some detail, as it highlights the difficulties of working with different funding sources, in this case the LEA and the MSC, while maintaining personal integrity and credibility with young people. The facts are these. In 1980 Wyre District Youth Service, on behalf of Lancashire County Council, entered into a contract with the MSC to provide 'life skills', off-the-job education for Youth Opportunities Programme trainees. Two tutors were engaged and, using full-time workers to work alongside them, they ran a rolling programme of two two-and-a-half-day residential courses, and two full-week courses for thirty trainees each six months. The workers were pleased at the access this work gave them to funds as well as to a group of young people they would not normally have contacted. The course objectives and programmes were submitted through the normal LEA channel for approval, and also sent to the MSC for information. The first problem was the residential programme on sex and gender education. The course was visited by two county advisers and the AEO, and the workers' argument that it was an essential part of the education of young men and women prevailed, after two meetings, four lengthy reports and solid support from the DEO.

The price was that course details and evaluative reports had to be sent to the AEO, the County Adviser (Youth), and Area Adviser (Youth), the DEO, the Director of a Residential Centre, the Manager of the MSC (Lancashire) and the MSC Training Officer. It was rumoured that the MSC 'did not allow sex education' and that was why it was omitted from their literature. This was never stated to the workers on this occasion and the MSC seemed very satisfied with the work undertaken.

After the third series of courses it was decided to run a different residential course called 'Looking at Unemployment'. It was set up for fifteen young people who had been doing the previous courses, but were unemployed following a year of the YOP, and twelve young people who had completed the series of four courses, but were still 'YOP'. Details were sent to the County Adviser and the MSC Area Manager, both of whom approved the course. The intention was stated to use the course to help young people to complete a report on youth unemployment and perceptions of it as gleaned from members of the public in a street survey, interviews with a teacher, a journalist, a careers officer, a youth worker and a Job Centre manager, and that the report would be published and circulated to such people as the authors, that is, the young people, wished it to be sent. The only response was from a Senior Assistant Education Officer who wrote to the effect that 'Nothing must be published without prior LEA approval'.

The course ran. The young people wrote the report, which in the event was quite mild and said little more than what the local paper and *The Times Educational Supplement* were saying. Its conclusion was that everyone realised that youth unemployment was a problem, many people cared, but no one seemed to know what to do about it. The young people were proud of the report and notwithstanding the LEA instructions, the workers took the view that it was the young people's report (using LEA typing and paper) and that they had a right to send it to whoever they chose. The young people sent the report to, among others, the local newspaper, which ran a half-page article on it. Within five days the MSC had notified the LEA that it was withdrawing the contract, with no reason ever being given. Within ten days the matter had to be explained to the Chief Assistant Education Officer, who fortunately took a liberal view of the matter and which was closed with a warning letter. The end result was that with the withdrawal of the MSC contract the work of the district was in total disarray as the workers had become dependent on that funding and access for 50–70 per cent of their work. It was fortunate that the MSC employee had just been appointed to an LEA post so no one lost their job as a result of the contract withdrawal.

This taught the district two important lessions. Firstly, never to believe that funding sources could in the long term be used without strings, and secondly, never to become dependent on resources which could be withdrawn instantly and without explanation.

A second example of youth workers at risk is demonstrated by the Boys' Clubs' record of parting company with youth workers (leaders) who develop work in ways which is not acceptable to the Movement. CYWU fought five cases in a year on behalf of members of the union who were employed by Boys' Clubs and found themselves in employment difficulties after variously:

- 'working on the more artistic end of our type of work'
- developing 'athletics, canoeing and community involvement as part of his new curriculum activities . . . [rather than] . . . running successful football teams'
- running a football team 'as a social activity for local lads rather than those brought in because of footballing skill'
- attempting to start a girls' night.

What would seem to follow from the CYWU's experience is that continued employment with a Boys' Club may, in some places, be dependent on subscribing to a set of values and conditions which are not recorded, but are embodied in the traditions and management of the clubs.

If participation ever becomes a reality as opposed to a series of token gestures, then there will be a rapid rise in numbers of youth workers who find themselves in the high risk quadrant of the model shown in Figure 8.1. To advance youth work, both in terms of access to resources and in developing the work itself, youth workers have pressure on them as never before to be entrepreneurs. What is needed is to develop a model of entrepreneurialism which meets the following criteria. That it:

can be carried out both within a voluntary and local authority setting
assists the worker to minimise the risks involved
maximises the opportunity for effective youth work, without 'selling out the kids'.

The Wyre District Youth Team has gone some of the way towards developing a method for achieving this. The process was in part systematic, and in part desperate survival strategy. Much of the learning of where walls were was achieved by the simple practice of walking into them. Presumably other individuals and groups have experienced, or are currently suffering, similar problems. It would have been helpful to us to have had others' experiences to draw on, and the rest of this chapter is offered in that spirit. The first step was to work out a clear and easily statable set of principles which were acceptable to the full-time team of workers. This covered:

the relationship between all workers full-time, part-time and voluntary;
the relationship which we could offer to the young people;
accountability to a wide range of people including the LEA, the wider community, the young people and the team itself;
the youth work and curriculum.

In order not to exclude anyone, it was important that the principles were set out in terms free from jargon and mystique. From this base it was possible to develop a consistency which permeated the whole of the work – its curriculum, method, style, practice and priorities. The links between the objectives and the actions to meet those objectives are set out

OBJECTIVES

ACTIONS	Common principles	Consistency	Theoretical base	Good practice	Wide information base	Creditability with local community	Creditability with agency (LEA)	Accountability	Influence	Credibility with young people	Innovation
Meetings											
Team meetings	X	X	X								X
Management Committees				X		X	X	X	X		
District Youth Committee				X		X	X	X	X		
Working parties (policy)				X			X		X		
Working parties (curriculum)				X			X		X		
Youth Officer's Meetings				X			X	X	X		
Further Education Sub-committee				X					X		
Reporter writing.				X		X	X	X	X		
Staff development											
Courses			X	X							
Part-time worker training		X	X	X		X	X				X
Assessment		X		X							X
Recruitment of part-time workers						X		X	X		
Role of workers											
Full-time workers		X		X		X	X	X	X	X	X
Part-time workers		X		X		X	X	X	X	X	X
Practice											
Work review	X	X	X	X				X		X	X
Curriculum development				X	X		X				X
Curriculum relevant and acceptable to young people				X					X		
Inter-agency working (acceptable to young people)									X		
Wide consultation and participation						X	X	X		X	
Commenting on consultative documents							X		X		
Responding to agency requests							X	X	X		
Reading				X	X	X					
Bidding for funds/facilities							X	X			X

Figure 8.2   *Objectives and actions*

schematically in Figure 8.2. It is essential that all areas are progressed in an orchestrated way as they are bound together: all parts are interdependent. For example, in order to develop the curriculum area of political education it was necessary for full- and part-time workers to be committed to innovation and to be able to develop theory and practice from their own resources as well as from the work of others. They had to be able to work with young people, the committees, the wider community and the LEA, informing and consulting at every stage. Everyone had to be engaged in the process in order to make progress and for the service to be accountable. This could not have happened without a fair level of credibility in developing other curricular areas and a solid staff development practice to support workers.

The consistency has had a set of consequences, the most obvious being team membership. This is limited to people who can broadly accept the existing value system, which could have had a claustrophobic effect on the thinking of the team. In practice this negative effect has been counteracted by pressures and inputs from all sectors of the work, reviews and regular attendance at training events both local and national.

The second consequence is the need for regular team meetings, of the full- and part-time worker teams, in order to avoid 'the truth' being the prerogative of a very few workers, and to facilitate consistency, good practice and innovation. However, this is not a comfortable process as it forces the confrontation of issues and inconsistencies, provided the style is open and consultative. The advantage of working from a common ideological base within a consistent system is that any member of the team can speak with confidence in meetings, or take decisions in the knowledge that they will have team backing. This means that individuals have increased influence and also that if it becomes necessary it is possible to work at great speed with minimal consultation and so take opportunities for resources or access. But for this base, the team might have disintegrated under pressure. An example of this was that when the MSC withdrew the contract it was possible to produce a new development plan within three days. This was against a background of alternative employment being offered to two of the full-time workers, and possible disiplinary action. The plan has been the basis of the team's work for the past four years. Part of the practice has been carried forward from the MSC period and can be expressed as four areas of concern in an entrepreneurial model.

The entrepreneurs – the team

There is a high commitment to working as a team, with part-time workers as equal members. This has consequences for the full-time workers, who have moved away from face-to-face work with young people towards being trainers, supporters and servicers of the part-time workers, who carry out most of this work. Each team has its own character. What is important is for all team members to have a clear understanding of what they may reasonably expect of the team, and the team of them.

The Wyre team is a working one, not a team in which deep personal friendships are common. The functions of the team include personal support in working situations, planning, priority setting and co-ordination. Most importantly, it acts as a critical filter through which work, thinking and innovation is assessed. This insures that, as one member put it, 'not too much rubbish gets out, as we spot it first'. Another major function of the team is creativity, brought about by linking facts, problem solving, analysing, synthesising and developing new ideas. The workers within the team are not 'cloned'. The only things held in common are the agreed principles and practice of youth work. This diversity gives strength to the team, provides a huge pool of experience which can be drawn on and a wide information base on which to build. It gives flexibility and an increased ability to respond to new situations. The price of this style of working is the tension which results from the divergence of personal positions and team views.

The team's practice, as stated previously, is based on agreed principles and curricular areas. These are put into operation following the systematic model shown in Figure 8.3. Although this is a text-book approach the model is actually used in day-to-day practice and we find it helps us to be clear about what we are doing and why, and how far we are succeeding. It is a tool of the job, and not an exercise to keep 'others' happy; it also assists in the development of coherent practice. The effect of this method of working has been to lay the myth of some vague consensus model of the Youth Service which has existed in many people's minds since the Albermarle Report of 1960.

The team declares itself to be about young people having the opportunity to acquire power and access through the process

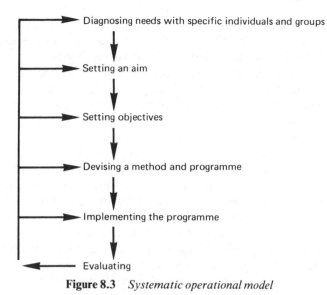

Figure 8.3 *Systematic operational model*

of education. This education is specific. It covers core skills of communication, decision-making, relating to people and knowing oneself. The curricular areas are participation and political education, sex and gender education, work with women, use of the outdoors, developing creativity, anti-prejudice work and life skills. This, continuing the entrepreneurial theme, means that the team is in competition with suppliers of other youth services, such as Youth Service (leisure), Youth Service (social services), Youth Service (containment) and Youth Service (fitting people into society). It follows that we have to have a product which is relevant and acceptable to the market (young people) and to the backers and bankers (the LEA and the wider community).

The market – young people and the wider community

It is vital that the young people feel that they are not being exploited or sold out, but are being offered a relevant service over which they have some real and significant control. In pragmatic terms, youth work is dependent on young people being willing to be involved.

The majority of changes resulted from the fact that the team felt that certain forms of work were closed because they destroyed this credibility; equally, other areas were essential because they met the stated needs of young people. It will be useful to examine three examples of this in action. Firstly, withdrawal from school-based work on the issue of seeing young people as inexperienced adults rather than as children. At this period the three full-time youth workers were based in schools for one third of their work and engaged in working with groups of school leavers both residentially and non-residentially. The practice was to encourage the young people to question the value system in which they found themselves and to work with them towards establishing a system which they could justify to themselves and, which was reasonably consistent. That work demanded that young people were treated as responsible, if inexperienced, adults, capable of independent thought and action. The whole process led to conflict with schools over a multitude of minor matters. For example, could the young people go out of school unaccompanied? Did they have to return to be 'seen' before the lunch break? Could young people working in a youth centre in school time leave when the work was complete or must they stay until the official leaving time? Were matters discussed between a young person and a worker confidential to those two people? Were the youth workers encouraging ill discipline by suggesting that young people asked teachers for explanations of decisions? The young people were uncertain of our position, viewing us either as 'soft teachers' or people who said that they held certain beliefs but seemed always to be compromising them.

The team was never able to discuss these matters as a coherent whole with the schools and, without any consultations with the youth workers, local head teachers decided not to support residential school-leaver courses by refusing to release the young people to attend. This was the signal for the team to withdraw from school work, which they did within a term. They had no alternative bases and developed work from street contacts and through projects and residential courses. Severing the school link was a relief as it removed tension and allowed the team to work more effectively. It forced them to develop styles of education which were acceptable and relevant to young people without the enticement of offering something better than school, or a place with music and snooker.

A second example involved ceasing to work with the Careers Service on the real jobs issue. Initially the team attempted to work closely with the Careers Service as the workers felt, and still feel, that they should be working towards the same ends, playing a complementary part in helping people develop as young adults. As unemployment grew, and the number of government schemes increased, the two services grew apart. The Careers Service had a detailed knowledge of local situations, of which schemes were job replacement, which schemes were exploitative and which schemes were positive, yet there seemed to be a reluctance to act on behalf of the young people in these matters and a tendency to support the employers. Young people did not seem to be informed of their rights to refuse placements and were merely being fitted into 'the system'. The Careers Service appeared to be an agency which was helping to keep young people in a state of suspended adolescence, rather than helping them to develop into adults. Many of the young people with whom the team worked had a similar opinion of the Careers Service and it damaged the team's credibility with young people to be seen working alongside Careers Service workers. Contact is now limited to those areas and individuals where the two services work to a common end.

Working for real rather than token representation of young people in places where decisions affecting them are taken is the third example. There were two strands to this work. Firstly, the adults who could affect access had to be convinced of the need to involve young people and be prepared, and able, to modify their style so that the young people could participate freely. Secondly, the young people had to have skills and confidence to take the first steps. The Wyre District Youth Committee was of inestimable help here. The chairperson, a local councillor, was swiftly committed to young people's involvement and waived both the constitution and normal committee procedure to make sure that the young people's voices could be heard. Ten young people were appointed to the committee. Meetings became more of a forum than a committee and the business became that of acting as a pressure group for, and on behalf of, young people's issues. As a result of pressure from the District Youth Committee young people were included on police liaison committees and involved in meetings with a range of people with a measure of authority over their lives.

Finally, four independent youth councils were set up, clerked and advised by youth workers, but each with the right of totally independent action. In parallel with this, youth workers supported young people on youth management committees and persuaded chairpeople to waive the 'two young people only' rule to involve larger numbers of young people. User groups were formed in centres to take over some responsibility for the running of the centres. To support these young people a range of courses were run continually, based on the idea of a core of communication and decision-making coupled with the identification of live issues and the pursing of these issues by researching facts and presenting and arguing a case in order to achieve changes. Such issues have included reduced prices for UB40 holders in local leisure facilities, obtaining funding to convert a disused school into a youth and community centre and commenting on the limitations of the Youth Training Scheme and the role of the local in-school Careers Service. More than fifty young people actively participate in this way at any one time and they come from a huge range of backgrounds, experience and academic achievement. They are involved because they wish to be, not because they are selected by youth workers and committees. In no sense are they tools of the youth workers.

The team has still a long way to go down the road of participation, for example, we have only just started to involve young people in interviews for workers, both full- and part-time. However, the team has achieved expectations, both among young people and the wider community, that young people will participate.

Credibility with the wider community is as important as credibility with the young people. The community should have concern for the education offered to its young people and it is our duty to be accountable to them. It is equally important that sectors of the wider community with power do not prevent the access of young people to that power. This makes for permanent tension within the work and the team has consciously pursued policies to explain the work to the wider community and to involve people in the work and the decisions which surround it. A policy has developed of recruiting part-time workers from within the local community wherever possible, and not seeking to recruit from professions such as teaching, social work and probation. This has forged links within the community which could not have been developed in any other way. Additionally, it has expanded the knowledge and skill base of the team and brought in new thinking.

The development of practice which followed from the role relationship between full- and part-time workers included a commitment to part-time youth worker training and an effective local staff development policy. This has not yet been completely achieved. A large amount of effort has been put into developing a county-wide part-time youth worker training programme and pioneering part-time workers acting as tutors on the course. Attempts to achieve alternative routes to full-time qualifications have not so far met with success. This out-of-district work was essential in order to set up a county system which allowed Wyre to develop workers in line with the team's policy. It must be stressed that none of this activity was entered into cynically in order to build a safe base; it was begun as a result of normal practice. These factors were only recognised as important in the wider context as the work developed.

The team has sought to be accountable as a matter of principle. The practice has always been to declare intentions openly and to write honest reports. This takes a great deal of time. Gradually, people have come to understand what the team does, how it is done, that the workers report what happened and that they honour decisions once made. This has raised the team's credibility even among people who oppose their actions. It has helped to build support which extends into areas of the community where youth workers might expect to have no access. The result is that the teams bids for increased funding and facilities tend to have wide backing and con-sequently be viewed seriously and sympathetically. Further, it has in the long term reduced pressure on the practice. Visits and inspections have always been welcomed and people have felt no need to explore in order to discover if anything was being hidden. The price of this openness is that successes and failure are very public affairs.

The policies of accountability, real influence of the community on decision-making, involvement and staff recruitment have gradually paid off, assisted by the view that the team members are not seeking personal gain. Inevitably this credibility is patchy, in places it is absent and in many places no one knows of the team's existence!

The bankers – the LEA

To work effectively the confidence of the LEA, both officers and politicians, must be retained. Despite the fact that the Wyre District Youth Service is very small, many people within the whole range of departments know of its existence, because the team cause work to come on to their desks. It is important that the Youth Service is viewed sympathetically: the high profile of entrepreneurialism requires an effective marketing strategy and a positive image.

In order to create a good climate, and because it is an important way to progress work, the team seeks to contribute to all working parties, especially those based around policy, curriculum development and training. Comments are always made in response to all consultative documents and the team initiate discussion through papers and memos. The workers try to keep their administration in good order, responding to requests on time, keeping required records and completing returns. A bid is made for any additional resources that are available, making as well-prepared a case as time permits. The team members also try to be known as individuals, not just signatures on bits of paper, and so they quite often visit people rather than write to them, and they attend Further Education and Education committees as members of the public. The climate this creates, together with the development of good practice and active accountability, seems to make bids for funding and facilities more likely to succeed. This allows the team to develop practice without unacceptable constraints.

The competitors – strategies to limit their effect

The only tactic used is that of seeking influence. Influence, such as the team has, comes via the workers' credibility and through the system of consultative committees, unions and working parties. It comes from always being there, always contributing and always volunteering to work. The importance of the team back-up has already been explained. Thus, by influencing policy at all levels, district, local authority and national, it is possible to move policy to a point where the team's practice is in line with it, and therefore the practice needs no special protection. It is, then, the practice of others which is exposed. In order to work in this way it is helpful to have a wide knowledge of Youth Service matters as well as local government administration, regulations and practice. There is no easy way to gain this; it is a combination of extensive reading, listening to others and never being afraid to say, 'I'm sorry I don't understand that!'

Conclusion

At the beginning of the chapter a model of entrepreneurialism was offered, one factor of which was 'gains made in resources for young people'. There is only one cake, and there is competition for every crumb of it. Too often youth workers accept only the crumbs they are given and young people are almost never encouraged or helped to bid for a slice of the cake in their own right. The closing of the circle is to put the young people (the market) in direct contact with the LEA (the bankers). This is called participation! When this is achieved the young people, not the youth workers, are the entrepreneurs.

What are the implications of the entrepreneurial model, 'the organisation or management of an undertaking, assuming the risk for the sake of profit'? Certainly it is hard work, full of tensions between young people, the community, the funding agencies and the other priorities. It is stressful and if, and because, individuals care, they get hurt. However this is true of all models of youth work, so how is the entrepreneurial model different? It is different if the model used is high in risk. If risks are taken, then on occasion there are failures and the failures have consequences, both in personal terms and in terms of employment. Employers can use a range of strategies and sanctions to limit a worker's effectiveness if they deem it to be necessary; these range from withdrawing funding and co-operation, to removal from post. Therefore, before using this model each individual should be sure what level of risk they are prepared to accept and for how long and, before making any move, the risks should be considered and explored. It is too late to pull back once the process has started.

Finally, in a short chapter, it is easy to make it appear that work and development has been smooth, well-orchestrated, successful and harmonious. It has not been. This is no more than a distilation of learning from a process. To catalogue the failures, the mistakes and the disagreements would take a book which might well run into a second volume! In the last four years the team has increased its resources and personnel five-fold. The work is not heavily prescribed. Young people and the wider community are actively involved in the decision-making of the Service. There are a team of part-time workers who are second to none. The team has formulated local policy, significantly influenced county policy and just once or twice influenced national policies – and the work has really only just started.

9

Youth Workers as Character Builders: Constructing a Socialist Alternative

TONY TAYLOR

The rhetoric of youth work for two decades has proclaimed the death of character building as the guiding principle for work with young people, its traditions buried alongside Lord Baden-Powell and the end of the British Empire. Thus, at the beginning of this chapter, the reader might be preparing for a smug and sarcastic reflection on the eccentricity of a past practice, where young men were fighting fit, keeping their hands well away from their genitals and young women were busy preparing to be mothers, fit for little else. Indeed, within the serious attempt of Butters (1978) to analyse the historical development of the Youth Service he declares that a traditional leadership model has been transcended. Into its place of predominance have surged the person-centred and community-orientated perspectives fostered by Albemarle (HMSO, 1960) and Milson–Fairbairn (DES, 1969). Character building is dead, long live personal growth! And yet, if one works within and makes pilgrimage around youth work's historic sites of coercion and compliance, the real world tells a different tale. Although the world of moral discipline, God, Queen and Country has suffered much scorn from the likes of trendy liberal trainers (such as the author in the mid-1970s), it has resolutely retained its dominance over the arena of actual practice. Contrary to what liberal ideologies might wish to be true, character building, the indoctrination of obedience to the capitalist imperative, is alive and flourishing. Whilst youth work theory has suggested otherwise, youth work practice has not been thrown off course by the advent of Thatcherism – it had never really deserted those vaunted Victorian values.

This chapter attempts to shed some light on this state of affairs and to account for the strength of reactionary character building. In doing so, the feeble and co-opted challenge to conservatism's supremacy offered by the distraught liberal-cum-social democratic alliance of confused and caring youth workers (of which the author has been a willing and unwilling member for fifteen years or more) is noted. Consequently, the ever-pressing need to construct a self-conscious, confident, socialist opposition, theoretically rigorous, politically determined and efficiently organised is offered as a campaigning alternative. Engaging with youth workers in a critical dialogue about the possibility of a socialist alternative is an utter necessity. But saying this is a good deal easier than doing it.

An apparatus of social control

In beginning the enterprise, accounts need to be settled with Butters' analysis, which shifts from a functionalist interpretation of youth work's purpose to a voluntarist appraisal of how this state of affairs might be overcome. The Youth Service is characterised as an ideological state apparatus that seeks to inculcate normative practices into the daily lives of working-class young people, remedying deficits in the activities of the family, church, schooling, police and wider welfare institutions. Butters' conclusion is to propose that young women and men themselves, in a collective act of cultural self-emancipation, could break this stranglehold of control.

His historical account of the Youth Service argues that character building with its tactic of demanding deference to admirable models of behaviour has 'become disestablished', its heyday long past in the early 1900s. The promotion of good character through physical coercion, sexual restraint and dutiful obedience has been superseded by the three components comprising the cultural ensemble of the Social Education Repertoire (SER). Within the Repertoire, are discovered the person-centred practices of cultural pluralism (1930s to 1970s) – the doctrine of individual change; the functionalism of community development (late 1960s to 1970s) – the ameliora- tion of tensions in society; and a social democratic strategy of institutional reform (1890s to 1970s) – the mobilising of groups to effect structural change. Despite appearances, Butters argues that these three elements form a cohesive liberal humanist front, within which the expert professional plays a leading role. As such the sophisticated social engineering approaches of the SER stifle the prospect for change contained within his Radical paradigm, which celebrates the possibility of working-class young people as the vanguard of a cultural revolution.

However, Butters' vision stems not from the anti-intellectual tradition of ignorance cultivated so lovingly by the Right in youth work, but from the fact that he underestimates the strength of traditionalism, exaggerates the influence of liberal- ism and idealises the revolutionary possibility. Be this as it may, the spirit and political intention of his analysis are correct. A revolutionary socialist practice is sorely needed.

The reality of youth work practice

The compelling dilemma is that Butters' whole theoretical edifice is endangered by its foundation on the thin basis of what workers claim to be doing rather than a deep interrogation of concrete practice. Peeling away the layers of rhetoric, theory and practice from around youth work's hard core of policing and control reveals all manner of deception. Mark the gulf between what policy-makers, academics, trainers and officers promulgate and what it is usually like in the youth club. Thus, in youth work training, a great fuss is made about the client- centred strategy of non-intervention and about the hallowed skills of groupwork and counselling, whilst in the youth centre an inhibiting and insensitive authoritarian approach continues to prevail. This mismatch is confirmed by the workers' reluctance to admit what is really going on. Some workers perhaps wonder whether colleagues do have a high level of serious member participation, and do challenge consistently sexism and racism, whilst others are bogged down in money missing from the coffee bar and the toilets not working, or are so busy policing the building that they ignore the male-dominated pool table. In venturing an essay on transforming practice, it must be acknowledged that in the pressure cooker of day-to-day work, Baden-Powell seems to have a great deal more influence than Carl Rogers (1973).

The myth of the SER

If character-building has not been surpassed, where does this leave the SER? Given the space available in this argument, this chapter will have to skip lightly over the semi-conscious bodies of community development and institutional reform, for they appear only briefly on the youth work stage. They do not exist in the consistent form necessary for their promotion as central planks of the contemporary youth work platform.

Whatever the contradictions of their reformism, bent on the best possible deal under a beneficent welfare capitalism, their slogans of participation and political rights have been viewed with deep mistrust inside the Youth Service. Certainly, community development's emphasis on the democratic process has fuelled youth work's rhetorical fixation with young people's involvement. However, the road to young people's power remains strewn with martyred workers tripped up for traversing too quickly the participative path. In practice, whenever these two strands of activity have shown signs of real life, the bureaucratic guillotine has rapidly ended their existence (see, for example, Taylor and Ratcliffe, 1981, pp. 26–30). This significant and optimistic contradiction will be returned to in drawing up the socialist alternative, namely that these social democratic engineering approaches display a radical potential.

Its compassionate heart

Where Butters does put his finger on the pulse of the liberal opposition to character-building is in the cultural pluralist strand: 'the non-directive enabling of individuals towards self-actualisation' (ibid., p. 30). There is hardly a youth worker in Britain who hasn't groped his way through the group work experience, and nodded her head in empathy with the traumas it spawned. The aim of youth work training through the 1960s, 1970s and into the 1980s was, and is, to make psychologists of youth workers. Given liberalism's sanctification of the individual, its notion that ideas make the world go round and the illusory promise of post-war prosperity, this is not altogether surprising. Any young person not making the most of the endless opportunities proffered at that time was in need of support from a trained band of counsellors and group-workers. Thus youth workers have been bombarded with an eclectic pot-pourri of half-baked pieces of adolescent, social and humanistic psychology. This one-sided theoretical obsession proves profoundly anhistorical and spuriously apolitical. Within its discourse, society becomes a marginal abstraction, the social relations of power deemed irrelevant. What matters is getting inside one's own head and thence into other people's heads. Ironically, despite all its blather about individuality, this psychological perspective engages only with generalised individuals denied their class, gender and race, and makes a fetish of the style rather than the content of human practice.

The adulation heaped on Carl Rogers (1973) is significant. His theory of self translated into a counselling process has been widely proselytised. Despite its useful observations on the tactics of listening to and supporting people in crisis, it has failed the test of practice. Most workers have abandoned its idealism in the nitty-gritty of their endeavours, recognising its denial of the material constraints of human existence. They have chosen to give advice and opinion to working-class young women and men, who do not have a clear field within which to discover their authentic selves, hampered as they are at every turn by their social and political powerlessness. At their worst, Rogers and Co. have offered an ideological rationalisation in the name of care and compassion for political passivity. For counsellors – technicians in human relations – possess no answers and no analysis, merely facilitating the self-adjustment of the individual as if in a political vacuum. Workers seduced by this have been drained of confidence and reduced to ciphers of change. Within youth work, counselling and group work have been elevated to the status of philosophical and political principle, when in fact their proper place lies in the realm of potentially useful skills and techniques.

Leaving the musings of cultural pluralism, it has to be allowed that the ideology of personal growth disturbed the field, and, for a time, perturbed the character builders. However, shifting economic and political events have rendered liberalism, in the form of a discrete and oppositional ideology, compulsorily redundant. Indeed, liberalism is only feasible as a contestant in the hegemonic stakes during a period of relative prosperity. In the midst of the Thatcherite onslaught, liberalism survives only by accommodating to the Right and the forces of conservatism, which brings us to a consideration of character building itself. What does that upright figure standing on its own two feet look like?

The resilience and flexibility of conservatism

It is time to pay grudging respects to the vitality and stamina of the character-building design. All those cold showers and early morning runs have served their purpose: targeted on its goal of securing young people's acquiescence to the capitalist imperative, it has wormed its way deep into the structures of youth work. At the level of taking action and making decisions down at the club or project its ideas hold great sway. Its 'common-sense' explanation of how we experience our lives retains its power through a particular interpretation of oppression and exploitation as the natural outcome of an inevitable social order. This 'rich man in his castle, poor man at the gate' theme connects to the way in which youth workers and young people experience their relative power and powerlessness. Without experience of or access to oppositional understandings of the world, without a socialist 'good sense' to counter conservatism's 'common sense', it is all too easy for workers amid the hurly-burly of practice to capitulate to the only sensible option: the requirement to maintain order and control whatever the political consequences.

With their power base in the majority of male-orientated, activity-centred youth organisations, the character builders' resolve is to inculcate bourgeois norms, values and attitudes. The diet is one of endless competition and pot-hunting. Imposed discipline is necessary. Sexuality is heterosexuality. Male leaders pursue an education in manhood. Outdoor pursuits is the proving ground for true British grit. Mixed clubs are usually boys' clubs with a fringe female presence in the coffee bar or rendered 'invisible' in the toilets. 'Keeping them off the streets' and 'politics out of the club' remain popular slogans. The ideology of 'I'm only here to help individuals' in its optimistic mode and 'He/she's a bad 'un – ban 'em' in its negative form, is the mainstay of practice. A notion of individual inadequacy – 'blaming the victim' – remains a staple explanation whenever trouble rears its head.

To extend and reconstruct Eggleston's (1976) view, conservative youth work still sees a nation suffering from a deficit of discipline and devotion and is committed to expounding upon patriotism; the sanctity of the bourgeois family; the naturalness of competition; the inevitability of exploitation; white racial supremacy; a fear of sexuality; and a view of woman as either 'whore or madonna'. Creaming off those most devoted to its cause as the leadership of class collaboration, it desires to settle young working-class people down as responsible husbands, devoted wives, diligent workers in both production and reproduction, and as satisfied, but never quite satiated, customers and consumers.

Whilst the liberals wish away power relations and reduce the oppression of class, gender and race to a marginal matter of misguided predjudice, the conservatives have no such need for fantasy. The fact of class, gender and racial inequality is explained simply as the necessary consequence of the human condition. It is incumbent upon us to accept the terms of deals offered to us by the ruling class whatever our say in the drawing of the unequal social contract. Our duty and obligation as youth workers is to convince young people that the only course open to them is conformity and compliance, for all our sakes.

Yet if the reader is familiar with the youth work world, it is at this point that you might want to heckle from your armchair that socialist rhetoric has finally run out of control. Somewhat aggrieved, a reader might argue that they know many decent youth leaders who may be racist now and again, but who listen sensitively to a homeless young person; who may be virulently against trade unions, but wants to involve the members more in decision-making. And there is no choice but to allow the examples, for here's the rub. The conservative character-building model is not timeless and dogmatic. It retains its superiority through its co-option and incorporation of motifs from differing and interrelated ideologies. A moment's reflection shows that the social groupwork beloved of liberalism is the product of the American capitalist concern to develop more sophisticated management techniques; and that counselling is no longer the refuge of caring, balding humanists, but is utilised widely within the armed services.

Within mainstream youth work, the ideology guiding what workers do is a complicated interweaving of character building and pluralist threads. Members of a youth club staff team will occupy differing positions on a conservative–liberal spectrum of practices, ranging from 'hard' to 'wet' character builders. Individual workers themselves will pursue contradictory practices specific to particular situations in which they find themselves. It is not unusual for a worker to bark orders at one moment during an evening and half an hour later to be arguing for a non-interventionalist stance. As workers try to understand what is going on around them, bits of half-understood humanistic psychology vie for supremacy with pieces of behavioural modification. In the final analysis, however, the fixative holding this contradictory ragbag of ideas and practices together is the imperative of accommodation to capitalist, sexist and racist relations. The seizure of liberal notions by the forces of conservatism strips them of their liberatory content in the making of a persuasive and powerful mechanism for the maintenance of the status quo. Thus the successful club or project is one where individuals are helped as individuals and collective connections diverted into the cul-de-sac of camaraderie; where conflict is cooled down; where frustration is channelled into safe activities; where young men and women behave responsibly as prescribed; and where one Live Aid venture a year keeps everyone's conscience clear. Within even this eclectic mix there is no room for the resistance of young women, young blacks and the young proletariat. We will have to look elsewhere for the flickering flames of liberation. But we must not write off a relationship with a con-lib pact suffused with its own internal contradictions. There will be scope for intervention, provided we recognise that even when wearing a smiling face the slogan of con-lib is 'Life and Social Sub-servience'. Struggle and resistance by the young working class must be rooted out and routed.

All this leaves the committed liberals, the upholders of growth and non-intervention, in a stew. Unable on principle to join the ranks of the reactionaries, often cynical about and hypercritical of the political organisations of the class, caught in a time-warp of method and expectation, they have sought refuge in developmental work, intent on creating a service within the Service. This can be a precious cul-de-sac, however, a dead end. This form of liberal separatism is not to be confused in any immediate sense with the autonomous de-velopments in girls' work and black work grounded solidly in the real experience of sexism and racism. Without doubt, there will have to be an alliance with the liberals as the socialist strategy unfolds, but workers will live on their nerves through-out its course. The message to liberalism rings clear: your splendid slogans of liberty, equality and freedom are only realisable through the collective struggle for a socialist future.

A youthful Radical Paradigm

Running out of space means tarrying only a while with Butters' (1978) Radical Paradigm, which emphasises sub-cultural resis-tance and the leading role of working-class young people. There is more than a hint of romanticising the deviant here and a large dose of the Frankfurt School's historical disillusion-ment with the revolutionary capabilities of the working-class, embodied in Marcuse's (1964) pessimistic picture of mon-olithic manipulation in advanced industrial society and his flight of fancy about revolutionary students. Ironically, But-ters makes no reference in his vision to the radical develop-ments embodied in girls' work and the growth of independent black groups which might have strengthened his scenario. The principal reason for this absence is striking, namely that these black and feminist prefigurative political practices owe little or nothing to the outpourings of either part-time or full-time youth work training courses. Given that Butters used training as the mirror of the Service, he was always likely to miss the most profound practical developments. Certainly though, any plausible socialist strategy must beware Butters' focus on the revolutionary potential of the young proletariat and engage seriously with the enormous impact of feminist and black politics upon the white, male constituency in youth work.

A socialist opposition

In the face of a renewed and hardened version of conservatism; in the light of liberalism's demise, its shallow roots strangled in the collapsed soil of the social democratic consensus, a radical opposition is required, one which asserts the goal of transforming social relations; the achievement of socialism. Within youth work, the task is to establish a socialist consciousness in argument with and activity alongside working-class black and white young women and men. Through this process, workers aspire to play a part in the metamorphosis of the class from being defensive and confused 'in itself' to being able to act 'for itself' as the self-conscious agency for political change (Marx, 1970). Specifically in terms of the Youth Service, workers have to fight for the legitimacy of a socialist youth work pactice. Such an ambitious enterprise demands the working-out of a political programme of action and the creation of a disciplined form of organisation. Socialists in youth work do not have much choice in the matter. If workers are serious about their rhetoric, they have to come together to educate, agitate and organise. In preparation for this necessary step, the following interrelated themes are offered as an initial contribution to the collective and comradely debate.

Theory and practice

Without socialist theory, there can be no socialist practice and vice versa. Strengthening the theoretical grasp goes hand in hand with developing a practical grip on affairs. Indeed, the opportunity to delve into political contradiction with young people happens most frequently in everyday occurrences across coffee bars or in minibuses, when, on their terms, political questions are raised. These are the potential moments of critical dialogue, where the young people's experience is engaged and brought to interaction with the workers' socialist analysis, the rigorous endeavour to see below the appearance of things in uncovering the roots of oppression. Precisely because the workers' side of the dialogue depends on understanding 'what's going on behind the scenes', they are obliged to study, for example, the dynamics of the capitalist economy, the nature of the welfare state or the roots of racism and sexism, at the same time as being immersed in the living struggles of the class. The socialist enterprise falls at the first hurdle if workers are too ignorant to enter into political argument with young women and men.

Acting rationally

In stimulating the critical dialogue, socialist workers have to recognise their failure to ground individual practices in the material circumstances of people's lives. A socialist theory of personality is missing; a developed comprehension of individual and social interaction. Testimony to this state of affairs is provided by the sight and sound of the ranting socialist dogmatist and by the movement's tendency, in the absence of theory, to dismiss those who disagree as diseased and beyond redemption – a perverse interpretation of false consciousness as innate insanity. Against such a reactionary, biologistic perspective, workers have to nourish an understanding of men and women as rational actors, making the most sensible decisions possible given their circumstances and the ideas available to them. Working-class young people are thinking beings trying to make sense of their situation, but constrained by their place in the social relations of class, gender and race (see Sève, 1978; Leonard, 1984; Ashcroft, 1981 and Taylor, 1981). From the perspective of this chapter, such optimistic insight informs the workers' efforts to enable individuals to recognise the very socialist practices, which can change irrevocably the material circumstances. Such a youth work strategy will be founded on promoting socialist ideas as the liberatory means of looking at experiences and on making participation a priority in collective action, within the essential consciousness-raising process of political struggle.

Socialist socialisation

A youth worker's awesome job is to socialise, or more appropriately, politicise young people into the morality of collective responsibility and obligation, into a recognition of the justice of equality between black and white, male and female, homosexual and heterosexual, disabled and able-bodied, into a commitment to the class struggle. Socialisation has suffered a bad, radical press, most tellingly at the hands of feminism, but within youth work, it is the feminists more than anyone else who have countered patriarchal socialisation with the alternative of girls' work, the building of anti-sexist practices and the rediscovery of the lost traditions of women's struggle. Socialists must learn from this telling resistance and create their own prefigurative practices. Thus the concrete ways in which workers relate to young men and women; to one another as workers; to the methods utilised to make decisions; to individuals' willingness to explore the contradictions of actions and position as state workers; our practices as fallible human beings struggling with our racism; our conspicuous involvement in political struggle, this rich tapestry and more will be the everyday content of a socialist model.

To embark on such a perspective requires a confidence which clashes with the taken-for-granted state of uncertainty, adopted as a matter of course by so many liberal and radical workers. It is time to cast off the cover of confusion as the hiding place from clarity and commitment. Now is the moment to desist from all that indulgent agonising about whether youth workers have the right to impose their views on young people. The working-class young women and men with whom youth workers work have never been mindless dopes meekly awaiting their weekly visit to the local brain wash. If our socialist ideas do not connect to their life experiences, they will be put aside in favour of those notions which make more sense. As an alternative explanation, socialism faces an uphill struggle in competition with the ideas of the class that is 'the ruling material force and, at the same time, its ruling intellectual force' (Marx and Engels, 1970, p. 64). Ruling-class ideology is, of course, never monolithically triumphant and as workers strive daily within its contradictions they have no need to make life even harder by imposing indulgent self-censorship couched as 'who am I to tell anyone else what to do?' This is relativism oft cloaked as radicalism, which is the very antithesis of a committed, politicised practice.

A socialist programme

If workers are to move forward together rather than indulge in individual acts of conscience, a socialist manifesto is necessary. There would be a need for 'bridging' demands, which would seek in their construction to link the immediate needs of the situation with the necessary objective of socialist transformation. Such an approach would treat the short-term goal with proper seriousness, but would always look to going beyond the immediate in posing the questions of 'who has power and in whose interests is it exerted?' and 'how might we challenge fundamentally the power of the capitalist state?' (Trotsky, 1975). Thus, in facing the exploitation of young men and women on Youth Training Schemes, we would have to investigate the connections between a call for trade union rights and a rate of pay for work done; the Manpower Services Commission's role in the capitalist strategy of driving down wage levels and restructuring the workforce; demands for real jobs and genuine training; and the necessity of a socialist planned economy. In relation to the impact of girls' work, a socialist policy, which recognises the importance of resources for work with young women, is cautious about anti-sexist work with young men in the context of a male orientated service, but which argues with feminists about the need for a united alliance in the wider struggle of the young working-class, would need to be established. In this context 'autonomy but not separatism' would be called for, proposing that the right to autonomy of women within the overall movement of the oppressed is crucial, but that a separatism divorced from this holistic force, whilst it demands our respect, is finally antagonistic to the socialist project.

Grappling with dilemmas of such sensitive hues illustrates the necessity of working out within workers' own critical dialogue the manifesto's content and direction. Certainly programmatic guidance is needed in relation to a host of issues – black independence and anti-racist practice; the content and method of youth work training and practice; relationships with the youth work unions, with the Labour Party, Left groupings and their young socialist offspring; the potential of community work approaches; and, in the area of institutional reform, the prospects for municipal socialism. In the case of the latter, is there more room for manoeuvre in working for a Labour council with Left credentials, and how does this compare with possibilities in Tory-controlled settings? It has been argued that a serious socialist youth work trajectory would aspire to recruiting workers into specific Labour authorities, where political support for radical ventures is at its strongest. In the crucial area of credibility in the field, it can only be noted in passing that the materialist theory of individuality opens up the possibility for the Left of filling the vacuum vacated by the discredited ideas of counselling with sets of radical tips and cues for practice, which speak directly to the complexity of solidly supporting young working-class women and men. Certainly, the articulation of a clear-sighted programme would be liberating rather than inhibiting to youth workers' practice. Compare the thought of entering a committee meeting with a socialist sense of purpose based on collective argument, and the usual situation of operating off the top of the individual's head, praying that a gut-level response is adequate. It goes without saying, yet needs saying loudly, that any such socialist manifesto would be constantly open to revision and criticism.

A united front

Throughout the unfolding of workers' socialist practice, they would be in the business of making alliances and opening up conversations with other groups within youth work. Indeed, thus far, the progressive end of youth work appears as one great Popular Front, within which workers maintain a spurious unity on the basis of the lowest consensual point of agreement. Within such a broad alliance, workers keep their political mouths shut for fear of upsetting a delicate balance of forces which is so sensitively poised that it has rarely stood solid on any account. Thus socialism is hidden for short-term gain and in the process is abandoned by workers. In contrast to this interpretation of alliance, the United Front perspective allows workers to argue politically with, for example, liberals, feminists and black activists, for a socialist strategy, but commits them to unity of action after the internal debate, even if the socialist argument has fallen by the wayside. The only exception would be if the alliance's strategy is in flagrant contradiction with workers' socialist principles, for instance in the mounting of a racist campaign, and then workers would explain fully their break from such a bloc of forces.

In speculating upon programmes and alliances, and the relationship of a socialist youth work to the wider struggle against oppression, 'organised Labour' is the key agency in unlocking the possibility of closing the door on capitalist relations. This is not a matter of moral choice, that those collectivised at the point of production are somehow of a superior order to, say, women individuated at the point of reproduction or to the isolated young unemployed (see Anderson 1983, pp. 89–94; Miliband, 1985). To underline the specific structural relation of 'organised labour' to capital is not to suggest that waged workers can do it alone. Indeed, the fact of working-class young people's fragile relation to 'organised labour', given the level of youth unemployment, confirms socialist youth work's importance in creating connections between the varying constituencies of a proletariat, often divided by age, gender and race. Preparing a potion powerful enough to render capitalism unconscious requires the conscious mixture of all elements within the working class, not the least young women and men, with the yeast of 'organised labour'. Youth, women and blacks will not succeed in their historic quest for emancipation without the rest of the class. And the rest of the class has no chance without them!

A plea for organisation

Whether or not anything is done about any of the above hinges on the matter of organisation. As things stand, socialists in youth work are scattered and fragmented. Some workers are collectivised through their unions, but a grouping is needed which transcends the limitations of trade unionism. It is within workers' compass to build a socialist youth workers' organisation – human beings, including youth workers, make the world as much as it makes them. If youth workers respond to this particular historical task, their organised intervention into the dominant ideas and practices of reactionary youth work has the potential to shift the balance of forces in favour of the young working class. In this sense, 'the coincidence of the changing of circumstances and of human activity or self-changing can be conceived and rationally understood only as *revolutionary practice*' (Marx, 1970, p. 121, emphasis as in the original).

To end on a note that echoes the motifs of conservative character-building and, hopefully, recuperates them for the socialist cause. A consequence of the argument for confidence and the superior sense of socialist ideas is the proposal that workers have a leadership to offer in youth work. This is not a leadership good for all times and all places, nor is the only thing standing between youth workers and an advanced socialist practice the absence of leadership. Social and political relations are more complex than that reduction allows. But socialists in youth work should not duck their collective responsibility to lead the building of a revolutionary resistance to the onslaught upon the young working class. It is an honour and a duty to call oneself a socialist, to be a character builder of emancipation and liberation.

Postscript

Further reflection on completing the chapter suggests the following belated points. The analysis of character building and its liberal opponent lacks, perhaps, a sufficient sense of contradiction, bordering on simplistic caricature. In particular this criticism stresses the failure to mark seriously the internal inconsistencies of social democratic ideology and its radical potential. By and large, this charge is rejected. The chapter does acknowledge the contradictory nature of liberalism, but is not willing in the name of contradiction to capitulate to the reformism of social democracy. There is a qualitative world of difference between, on the one hand, floundering inside social democracy in a ceaseless quest to discover anew the seeds of its transformation and, on the other, entering its corridors from outside, armed with the very revolutionary socialist theory, which is the outcome of the historical struggle to transcend the limitations of both conservative and liberal bourgeois thought. The latter is no less capable than the former of engaging on a day-to-day basis with the positive aspects of social democracy and is far more able to resist collusion and incorporation into the capitalist charade.

To continue the inevitable emphasis on contradiction, a major weakness of the section on a socialist alternative is its assumption about the oppositional potential of being a state worker. During the last decade a focus on the importance of recognising prefigurative spaces in the state's activities has proved enormously attractive to radical youth workers. It has provided a progressive rationale for their frenetic commitment to the job. The influence of the 'In and Against the State' (London–Edinburgh Return Group, 1980) argument can be perceived in the optimistic framework for a socialist practice. However, the problem with weighting one-sidedly the contradictions of the capitalist state is that it romanticises and exaggerates the concrete possibility of a subversive socialist enterprise. In the final analysis, it is to lose sight of the bourgeois state as the instrument of capital. The reader may well have spotted other signs of this reformist malaise in the fleeting allusion to the possibilities of municipal socialism.

None of this is to suggest a withdrawal of the principal theme in the argument; the need for a purposeful, oppositional socialist youth work practice; but it is to propose caution about the idealism to be found scattered hither and thither within the chapter, exemplified by the call for a socialist youth workers' organisation. This is a gesture towards a collective form with little substance in the reality of workers' lives. More soberly, the idea of socialist workers sharpening their intervention into the myriad of major and minor moments of interaction, which are the substance of practice, must be defended. And the critical need for socialist workers and officers to caucus and organise on a local level around a programme of action must be underlined. However, on a grander scale, the genuine reference point for a wider collectivity will be a youth workers' trade union. The trade unionism should help cement youth workers' recognition of the limited aspirations of socialist youth work itself. Through collective support for one another as workers, they should make sure that their practice does not so exhaust them that they are incapable of a deep and consistent relationship with the political activity of the class. In tempering the socialist character, for workers and young people alike, there is no substitute for the class struggle itself.

Notes on the Contributors

Frank Booton is a lecturer in youth and community work at Sunderland Polytechnic.

Bruce Britton was employed as a youth/social worker at the Pilton Youth Programme in Edinburgh until October 1984. He currently works as a training and development officer for the Save the Children Fund in Newcastle-upon-Tyne.

Anne Foreman has worked as a centre-based youth and community worker since 1982 in the London Boroughs of Sutton and Kingston. She trained at Bradford and Ilkley Community College after several years' experience as an unqualified community worker. She is an active member of CYWU and is Chair of the Surrey Branch.

Gina Ingram has worked as a youth officer in the Wyre District of Lancashire since 1977, having previously worked as a youth worker in Essex and the Isle of Wight.

Tony Jeffs is a lecturer in social policy at Newcastle Polytechnic. He is editor of *Youth and Policy*.

Fran Lacey has worked as a neighbourhood youth worker in London for five years and was previously a detached youth worker in Leicester. She is currently involved in training and non-managerial supervision on a freelance basis.

Norman Powell started working life as a schoolteacher and has eight years' experience as a youth worker in the voluntary sector. He is currently employed by the Save the Children Fund

151

in Sunderland on an intensive intermediate treatment project aimed at diverting young people from custody.

Bill Rosseter was youth worker at the Up Town Coffee Bar, Aylesbury for four years. He now works in the Youth Information Service, part of the City Centre Project, at Milton Keynes.

Mark Smith is a tutor at the YMCA National College.

Carol Stone has worked in a variety of settings in youth and community work, including school-based and neighbourhood work. She is currently employed by Manchester City Council as a community education worker and is committed to developing a participative, neighbourhood-based service. She is active both locally and nationally in CYWU.

Tony Taylor currently works as a district youth and community education officer for Derbyshire County Council. In the past he has worked as a training officer for the Youth Service in Wigan and Leicestershire. He is active in CYWU and a member of it's Broad Left Caucus.

John Teasdale has worked as a teacher and youth worker and is currently working as a probation officer with Northumberland Probation Service. He was involved in the setting up of a local law centre and is a member of the *Youth and Policy* editorial group.

Bibliography

Anderson, P. (1983) *In the Tracks of Historical Materialism*, London, Verso.

Ashcroft, R. (1981) 'Conceptions of the Individual and Client in Social Science and Social Work', University of Bradford, unpublished.

Blegg, H. (1985) 'Reparation and Juvenile Justice', *British Journal of Criminology*.

Bolger, S. and Scott, D. (1984) *Starting from Strengths*, Leicester, NYB.

Britton, B. (1983) 'The Politics of the Possible', in Jordan, B. and Parton, N. (eds) *The Political Dimensions of Social Work*, Oxford, Basil Blackwell.

Butters, S. (1978) *Realities of Training – a review of adults who volunteer to work in the youth and community service*, Leicester, NYB.

Calouste Gulbenkian Foundation (1973) *Current Issues in Community Work. A Study by the Community Work Group*, London, Routledge & Kegan Paul.

Christie, N. (1977) 'Conflicts as Property', *British Journal of Criminology*.

DES (1969) *Youth and Community Work in the 70's* (The Milson–Fairbairn Report), London, HMSO.

DES (1983) *Young People in the 80's. A Survey*, London, HMSO.

Davies, B. (1976) *Part-time youth work in an industrial town*, Leicester, NYB.

Eggleston, J. (1976) *Adolescence and Community – The Youth Service in Britain*, London, Edward Arnold.

Hill, L. (1976) 'Counselling in Wandsworth', in Furedi, V. (ed.) *Working with Adolescents*, Leicester, NYB.

HMSO (1960) *The Youth Service in England and Wales* (The Albemarle Report), London.

HMSO (1981) *Report of the Parliamentary All Party Penal Affairs Committee*, London.

HMSO (1982) *Experience and Participation. Report of the Review Group on the Youth Service in England* (The Thompson Report) London.

HMSO (1983) *Criminal Statistics in England and Wales*, London.

Home Office (1982) *British Crime Survey*, London, HMSO.

Home Office (1983) *British Crime Survey*, London, HMSO.

Joint Negotiating Committee (Annual) Report for Youth Workers and Community Centre Wardens, London, Councils and Education Press Ltd.

153

154 *Bibliography*

Kuenstler, P. (ed.) (1955) *Social Group Work*, London, Faber.
Labour Research, vol. 74, no. 5, May 1985, pp. 146–147.
Lea, J. and Young, J. (1984) *What Is To Be Done About Law and Order?*, London, Penguin.
Leonard, P. (1984) *Personality and Ideology*, London, Macmillan.
Lerman, P. (1975) *Community Treatment and Social Control. A Critical Analysis of Juvenile Correction Policy*, Chicago, Chicago University Press.
London–Edinburgh Weekend Return Group (1980) *In and Against the State*, London, Pluto Press.
Marcuse, H. (1964) *One-dimensional Man*, London, Routledge & Kegan Paul.
Marx, K. (undated) *The Poverty of Philosophy*, Moscow, Progress.
Marx, K. and Engels, F. (1970) *The German Ideology*, London, Lawrence & Wishart.
Miliband, R. (1985) 'Class and Social Politics', *Socialist Society*, May/June.
NACRO (1985) *Juvenile Crime Briefing*, London.
National Council for Civil Liberties (undated) *NCCL Factsheets*, London.
Osborn, S. G. and West, D. J. (1980) 'Do Young Delinquents Really Reform?', *Journal of Adolescence*, vol. 3, pp. 99–114.
Pilton Youth Programme (1984) *Pilton Youth Programme Report*, Edinburgh.
Rogers, C. (1973) *Client-Centred Therapy*, London, Constable.
Rutherford, A. (1985) Unpublished Paper, University of Southampton.
Rutherford, A. (1985) *Training Anthology*, Yorkshire and Humberside IT Association.
Sève, L. (1978) *Man in Marxist Theory and the Psychology of Personality*, Brighton, Harvester Press.
Shamoon, S. (1985) 'Executives Beware' in *The Observer*, 30 September 1985.
Smith, D. R. (1984) *GREA Today: Gone Tomorrow? An Analysis of the Public Funding of Youth Work 1981/2 to 1984/5*, Leicester, NCVYS.
Smith, M. (1982) *Creators not Consumers – rediscovering social education*, Leicester, NAYC Publications, 2nd ed.
Stead, B. and Britton, B. (1984) *Youth Work in Scotland: 'An Alternative View'*, Edinburgh, Youth Action Charter.
Strathclyde Regional Council (1984) *Working with Young People*, Glasgow.
Taylor, T. (1981) 'Towards a Radical Practice', University of Bradford, unpublished.
Taylor, T. and Ratcliffe, R. (1981) 'Stuttering Steps in Political Education', *Schooling and Culture*, no. 9.
Thomas, D.N. (1983) *The Making of Community Work*, London, George Allen & Unwin.
Thorpe, D. *et al.* (1980) *Out of Care*, London, George Allen and Unwin.
Trotsky, L. (1975) *The Transitional Programme for Socialist Revolution*, New York, Pathfinder.
Ward, D. (ed.) (1982) *Give 'Em a Break. Social action by young people at risk and in trouble*, Leicester, NYB.

Whyte, W. H. (1960) *The Organization Man*, Harmondsworth, Penguin.
Wright, M. (1982) *Making Good – Prisons, Punishment and Beyond*, London, Hutchinson.

Index

158   *Index*